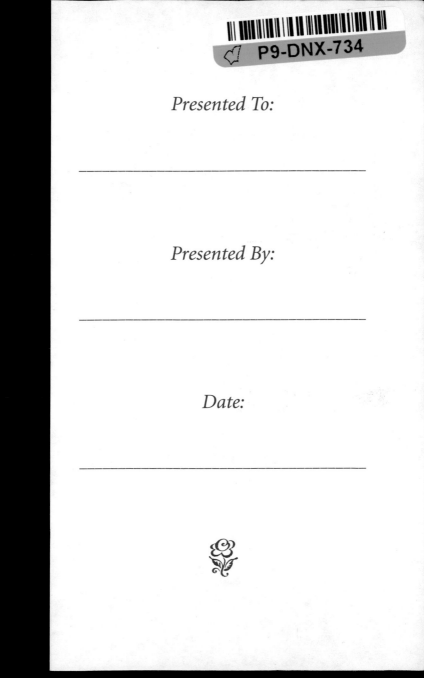

Presented To:

_____

Presented By:

_____

Date:

_____

God's Little Devotional Book
for Women

Honor Books
Colorado Springs, Colorado

God's Little Devotional Book for Women
ISBN 1-56292-212-2
Copyright © 1996, 2002 by Honor Books, Inc.
4050 Lee Vance View
Colorado Springs, CO 80918

Manuscript prepared by W.B. Freeman Concepts,
Tulsa, Oklahoma

God's Little Devotional Book for Women

Introduction

The devotionals in this book have been selected to provide a *pick-me-up* for your day. In the same way a snack or beverage gives you a burst of physical energy, these devotionals are snacks for the soul, awakening you to new insights about yourself and your relationships with family, friends, and colleagues. They will encourage you in your daily walk with God and will serve as a source of motivation as you accomplish your goals and fulfill your dreams.

Our hope is that the material in this book will remind you of God's promise—He is always near. Whether your heart is crying for comfort, protection, an expanded outlook, or direction, through these pages you will see He is both willing and eager to draw you closer to Himself, shield you from harm, comfort you with His presence, and encourage you with His Word.

Do you need a *pick-me-up* today? Then these devotionals are for *you!*

*My job is to take care
of the possible and trust
God with the impossible.*

*D*r. Amanda Whitworth was frustrated as
she crept up a hill with eight cars in front of her.
They were stuck behind a slow-moving truck,
and she was in a hurry. Amanda's last patient had
needed more attention than was allotted for
regular examinations, and she was late leaving to
pick up her daughter from day-school. Now she
breathed a prayer that she would not be late
again. It would be her third time, and because
the day-school did not tolerate parental tardi-
ness, she would have to make new arrangements
for Allie's afternoon care.

Amanda silently fumed at the truck's
progress. No one dared pass the truck on the
long hill, as it was impossible to see oncoming
cars around it. Suddenly, the truck driver waved

his hand indicating that all was clear ahead. As Amanda zipped past him, it occurred to her that this man was probably a stranger to all who passed him—yet nine people trusted their lives and the lives of their families to this man.

What a tremendous picture of how we do all we can do and then must trust even the smallest details of our lives to the care of God, who is a loving Heavenly Father. How comforting to know He can always see exactly what's ahead!

They that know thy name will put their trust in thee: for thou, LORD, hast not forsaken them that seek thee.

PSALM 9:10

When Mother Teresa received her Nobel Prize she was asked, "What can we do to promote world peace?" She replied, "Go home and love your family."

"The family," says Mother Teresa, "is the place to learn Jesus. God has sent the family—together as husband and wife and children—to be His love."

In *Words to Love By,* Mother Teresa writes, "Once a lady came to me in great sorrow and told me that her daughter had lost her husband and a child. All the daughter's hatreds had turned on the mother. She wouldn't even see the mother.

"So I said, 'Now you think a bit about the little things that your daughter liked when she was a child. Maybe flowers or a special food. Try to give her some of these things without looking for a return.'

"And she started doing some of these things, like putting the daughter's favorite flower on the table, or leaving a beautiful piece of cloth for her. And she did not look for a return from the daughter.

Several days later the daughter said, 'Mommy, come. I love you. I want you.'

"It was very beautiful.

"By being reminded of the joy of childhood, the daughter reconnected with her family life. She must have had a happy childhood to go back to the joy and happiness of her mother's love."[1]

Let love and faithfulness never leave you; bind them around your neck, write them on the tablet of your heart.

PROVERBS 3:3 NIV

You are never so high as when you are on your knees.

On a stormy day, with two experienced guides, a woman climbed the Weisshorn in the Swiss Alps. As they neared the peak, the woman—exhilarated by the view before her—sprang forward and was almost blown away by a gust of wind. One of the guides caught her and pulled her down, saying, "On your knees, madam! You are safe here only on your knees."

We typically regard "on our knees" as the standard position for prayer, but talking to God isn't limited to any position. He can hear us, regardless.

Three Christian women were talking once about the "best" positions for prayer. One argued the importance of holding one's hands together and pointing them upward. The second advocated that prayer was best when one was stretched out on the floor. The third thought standing was better than kneeling. As they talked, a telephone repairman listened as he worked on a nearby phone system. Finally, he could contain himself no longer and interjected, "I have found that the most powerful prayer I ever made was while I was dangling upside down from a power pole, suspended forty feet above the ground."

The important thing is not your *position* of prayer, but the fact that you do pray!

Humble yourselves in the sight of the Lord, and he shall lift you up.

JAMES 4:10

Give your troubles to God:
He will be up all night anyway.

W_{hy} pray?

We pray because prayer opens up the flood-
gates of God's infinite grace and power to flow
toward the person in need. God can act without
prayer, but He chooses to operate within the
boundaries of human will and invitation. He
allows us to participate in His work on earth
with each prayer.

Leonard Ravenhill once said about prayer,
"One might estimate the weight of the world, tell
the size of the celestial city, count the stars of
heaven, measure the speed of lightning, and tell
the time of the rising and the setting of the
sun—but you cannot estimate prayer power.
Prayer is as vast as God because He is behind it.
Prayer is as mighty as God because He has committed Himself to answer it."

A sign in a cotton factory read: "If your threads get tangled, send for the foreman." One day a new worker got her threads tangled. The more she tried to disentangle them, the worse the situation grew. Finally, she sent for the foreman. He asked, "Why didn't you send for me earlier?" She replied, "I was doing my best." He answered, "No, your best would have been to send for me."

When we face a tough situation, our first response should be to ask for God's help. He longs to be our helper and to be fully involved in our lives.

He will not allow your foot to slip;
He who keeps you will not slumber.

PSALM 121:3 NASB

*We should seize every opportunity
to give encouragement.
Encouragement is
oxygen to the soul.*

*I*n *Especially for a Woman,* Ann Kiemel
Anderson writes in her unique style about her
sister: "Jan taught 3rd grade once, a long time
ago. One bright-eyed boy would stand at her
desk, watch her, talk to her, and all the while
wrapping his finger around a piece of her hair
into a little curl. He thought Jan was the shining
star in the night. Over & over, however, he did
poorly in his work assignments and daily quizzes.

"One day Jan stopped, looked at him, and
said, 'Rodney, you are very smart. You could be
doing so well in school. In fact, you are one of
my finest students . . . ' Before she could continue
to tell him that he should be doing much better

in school . . . he looked up at her with sober, large eyes:

"'I did not know that!'

"From that moment on, Rodney began to change. His papers were neater, cleaner and his spelling improved. He was one of her top students—all because she affirmed him. She told him something no one ever had before, and it changed his life."[2]

Nobody ever became ill or died from receiving too much genuine praise and encouragement. But who can count the wounded hearts, weary souls, and troubled minds that have resulted from their lack!

A man hath joy by the answer of his mouth: and a word spoken in due season, how good is it!

PROVERBS 15:23

You may give without loving, but you cannot love without giving.

Most authorities believe King David's Temple was built on Mount Moriah where Abraham was told to sacrifice Isaac. But there's another Hebrew legend that presents a different story.

The legend says that two brothers lived on adjoining farms which were divided from the peak to the base of the mountain. The younger brother lived alone, unmarried. The older brother had a large family.

One night during grain harvest, the older brother awoke and thought, *My brother is all alone. To cheer his heart, I will take some of my sheaves and lay them on his side of the field.*

At the same hour, the younger brother awoke and thought, *My brother has a large family and greater needs than I do. As he sleeps, I'll put some of my sheaves on his side of the field.* Each brother went out carrying sheaves to the other's field and met halfway. When they declared their intentions to each other, they dropped their sheaves and embraced. It is at that place, the legend claims, the Temple was built.

Whether this story is true or not, it exemplifies the best expression of love—*giving*. Giving is one of life's best relation-builders.

For God so loved the world, that he gave his only begotten Son, that whosoever believeth in him should not perish, but have everlasting life.

JOHN 3:16

*When I come to the end of my
rope, God is there to take over.*

*T*he end of our human abilities is our
opportunity to turn to God. But giving up our
independence to depend on God isn't necessarily
easy. We are often like the woman in this story
reported in the Los Angeles Times:

A screaming woman, trapped in a car dangling from a freeway transition road in East Los
Angeles, was rescued Saturday morning. . . . A
half dozen passing motorists stopped, grabbed
some ropes from out of their vehicles, tied the
ropes to the back of the woman's car, and hung
on until the fire units arrived. A ladder was
extended from below to help stabilize the car
while firefighters tied the vehicle to tow trucks
with cable and chains.

"Every time we would move the car," said one
rescuer, "she'd yell and scream. She was in pain."

It took almost two and a half hours for the passers-by, CHP officers, tow truck drivers, and firefighters—about twenty-five people in all—to secure the car and pull the woman to safety.

"It was kinda funny." L.A. County Fire Captain Ross Marshall recalled later. "She kept saying, 'I'll do it myself.'"[3]

He hath said, I will never leave thee, nor forsake thee.

HEBREWS 13:5

The Lord can do great things through those who don't care who gets the credit.

*U*ntil the time Jane learned she needed an operation, the question, "Who will take care of me if I get sick?" had only been hypothetical. As a single woman, she hadn't given much thought to how she would survive a major illness or operation. As it turned out, she found that she had a "loving menagerie of friends" who "cobbled together a schedule of ministry and then passed the baton from one to the next while I marveled at my good fortune."[4]

Stephanie was the ringmaster, the one by her side at the hospital, who also helped her check her incision and take showers. Bob drove up from Los Angeles with his dog to stay for a few days after she returned home. Peggy brought over Thai take-out food. Ann arrived with a bread machine and bags of groceries. She also made soup, mopped the kitchen floor, and did the laundry. Michelle brought mail from the office and drove her to doctors' appointments.

It was amazing to Jane that these various people hardly knew each other when they first began helping her, but by the time she recovered, they had all become friends.

Being a servant has wonderful rewards. Many times in our serving we receive much more than we ever gave away.

A man's pride shall bring him low: but honour shall uphold the humble in spirit.

PROVERBS 29:23

What sunshine is to flowers, smiles are to humanity. They are but trifles, to be sure, but, scattered along life's pathway, the good they do is inconceivable.

The practice of one particular church was to dismiss the children in the Sunday morning service just prior to the sermon. The children would all march forward in a make-shift processional and sing a song as they passed the pulpit on their way to hear a sermon prepared just for them. The pastor enjoyed this part of the service. He made it a point to smile at each child and to receive a smile in return.

To his surprise, one morning a curly-headed four-year-old girl ran out of the procession and threw herself into her mother's arms, sobbing deeply. The pastor sought out the mother after the service to see what had happened. The child had told her, "I smiled at God, but He didn't smile back."

The pastor's heart sank. He had failed to smile, and the child's joy had turned to torment.

We may think our smiles do not represent God to another person, but they just might! Genuine smiles are a sign of affirmation, appreciation, and love.

Your smile can bring hope and change the countenance of someone today. Give it a try.

A happy heart makes
the face cheerful.

PROVERBS 15:13 NIV

I regret often that I have spoken;
never that I have been silent.

*W*hen Western Union asked Thomas Edison to "name his price" for the ticker he had invented, he asked for several days to consider it. His wife suggested $20,000, but he thought such an amount was exorbitant.

At the appointed time he went to the meeting still unsure as to his sales price. When the official asked, "How much?" He tried to say $20,000, but the words just wouldn't come out of his mouth. The official finally broke the silence and asked, "Well, how about $100,000?"

Often silence allows others to say something better than we could have said ourselves! By keeping quiet, others will have a greater interest in our thoughts; then when we have an interested audience, our words will have greater impact.

The Bible tells us that even a fool may be thought of as wise when his mouth is kept shut. (Proverbs 17:28.) In that sense, silence can keep us from embarrassing ourselves. People may think we are smarter than we really are.

When you feel moved to express an opinion, weigh the impact of your words and keep this thought in mind, "The *less* said, the *best* said." We can't get in trouble for what we don't say. Like Edison, we might even benefit from our silence.

In the multitude of words there wanteth not sin: but he that refraineth his lips is wise.

PROVERBS 10:19

"I can forgive, but I cannot forget," is only another way of saying, "I will not forgive." Forgiveness ought to be like a canceled note—torn in two, and burned up, so that it never can be shown against one.

A man once had too much to drink at a party. First, he made a foolish spectacle of himself—even to the point of wearing the proverbial lampshade as a hat—and then he passed out. Friends helped his wife take him home and put him to bed. The next morning he was very remorseful and asked his wife to forgive him. She agreed to "forgive and forget" the incident.

As the months went by, however, the wife referred to the incident from time to time, always with a little note of ridicule and shame in her voice. Finally, the man grew weary of being reminded of his bad behavior and said, "I thought you were going to forgive and forget."

"I have forgiven and forgotten," the wife argued, "but I just don't want you to forget that I have forgiven and forgotten."

Once we have confronted an offender, we must remember nothing is gained from harboring unforgiveness in our hearts. Forgiveness requires a healing process inside us—to the point where we no longer feel any pain at the memory of what the other person did or said to injure us.

We "forget" when we no longer hurt! When you make a commitment to forgive another person, ask the Lord to heal you of the impact of that person's behavior on your life. Forgive, forget, and start living again.

Be ye kind one to another, tenderhearted, forgiving one another, even as God for Christ's sake hath forgiven you.

EPHESIANS 4:32

*Worry is like a rocking chair:
It gives you something to do,
but doesn't get you anywhere.*

*P*eople who continually worry about every detail of their lives are like a patient in a mental hospital who stood with her ear pressed against the wall.

"What are you doing?" an attendant asked with curiosity.

"Shhhh," the woman whispered, beckoning to the attendant to join her at the wall.

The attendant pressed her ear to the wall and stood there for several moments listening intently. "I can't hear anything," she said.

"No," the patient replied with a furrowed brow. "It's been like that all day!"

Some worry about what might be said. Others worry about what hasn't been said. Some worry about what might happen. Others worry about what hasn't happened which should have happened by now. Some worry about their futures, while others fret over the consequences of their past.

We were created to live abundant lives in our minds, our bodies, and our spirits. Like a flower we were meant to blossom, not to wither on the vine. Put Jesus in charge of your worries today and walk in newness of life!

Casting the whole of your care [all your anxieties, all your worries, all your concerns, once and for all] on Him; for He cares for you affectionately, and cares about you watchfully.

1 PETER 5:7 AMP

*Look around you and be
distressed, Look within
you and be depressed,
Look to Jesus and be at rest.*

*T*he 911 emergency system has amazing
capabilities. In most places in the United States, a
person need only dial those three numbers to be
instantly connected to a dispatcher. On a computer screen the dispatcher instantly sees the
caller's telephone number, address, and the name
under which the number is listed. Also listening
in on the call are police, fire, and paramedic
assistants. A caller need not say anything once
the call is made. Even rasping coughs and hyster-
ical cries have brought a quick response. The dispatcher knows where the call is coming from, and
help is sent.

At times, some situations in our lives are so desperate and our pain so deep we can only muster a 911 prayer to God. These are called "SOS prayers," and they often use the same words: "God, I need help!" God hears each one. He knows our names and every detail of the situations. Like a heavenly dispatcher, He will send precisely who is needed to assist us.

Also like a 911 dispatcher, our Heavenly Dispatcher may have some advice to sustain us through a crisis. Keep a listening ear and remember, help is on the way!

In my distress I cried unto the LORD, and he heard me.

PSALM 120:1

There is no greater love than the love that holds on where there seems nothing left to hold on to.

A family sailing trip almost turned into a tragedy when gale-force winds and towering waves threatened to swamp the family's vessel. Their frantic call to the Coast Guard brought two ships to their rescue. Unfortunately, the first ship had only a rope ladder, a means of evacuation too dangerous in such rough seas. Then the 900-foot tanker, James N. Sullivan, arrived. It shielded the sailboat until, after several hours of maneuvering, a set of stairs could be lowered from the side of the tanker to the sailboat.

Using a safety line, Bob and Sherry made the transfer in good order, as did their two young children. Then it was Grandmother Laurie's turn. Grandfather Dave passed her tether to Bob, but her harness got caught when she stepped across to the ladder. As the boats pulled apart, Laurie fell into the sea. With a surge of the waves, the boats came crashing back together. Dave was afraid to look—he knew that his beloved wife of thirty-three years could not swim, and even worse, he feared she may have been crushed as the boats collided. Nevertheless, he clung to the tether, refusing to let go. Grandmother later explained, "That's the only reason I'm here."

No matter how troubled the seas of life may become, hold on to the tether with your love. A life will be saved because you trusted God for the impossible!

Love never fails [never fades out or becomes obsolete or comes to an end.]

I CORINTHIANS 13:8 AMP

Daily prayers will diminish your cares.

*M*any children learn to count on their fingers, but a nurse once taught a child to pray on his fingers. This was her method:

Your thumb is the digit nearest to your heart, so pray first for those who are closest to you. Your own needs, of course, should be included, as well as those of your beloved family and friends.

The second finger is the one used for pointing. Pray for those who point you toward the truth, whether at church or school. Pray for your teachers, mentors, pastors, and those who inspire your faith.

The third finger is the tallest. Let it stand for the leaders in every sphere of life. Pray for those in authority—both within the body of Christ and those who hold office in various areas of government.

The fourth finger is the weakest, as every pianist knows. Let it stand for those who are in trouble and pain—the sick, injured, abused, wounded, or hurt.

The little finger is the smallest. Let it stand for those who often go unnoticed, including those who suffer abuse and deprivation.

What a simple and wonderful reminder as we pray! What a great tool to use in teaching children how to pray for themselves and others.

Evening, and morning, and at noon, will I pray, and cry aloud: and he shall hear my voice.

PSALM 55:17

Be like a postage stamp—stick to one thing till you get there.

*A*ll her life, Veronica worked in jobs that served other people but gave her little personal satisfaction. As a young girl, she missed a lot of school to take care of her younger siblings and help with the family business. Consequently, she never learned to read.

After getting married, she worked as a cook in a restaurant, memorizing ingredient labels and recipes to conceal her illiteracy. Every day she lived in fear of making a mistake, while dreaming of one day being able to read.

A serious illness put Veronica in the hospital and then at home for a long recovery. Her health improved some, but not enough for her to go back to work. She saw this time as her opportunity to learn to read and enrolled in the adult reading program.

Veronica's new reading skills boosted her confidence, and she got involved in her church and in organizing community activities. She wrote a prize-winning cookbook and became a local celebrity.

Veronica never let go of her dream while working hard wherever she found herself. In the end, her dreams were realized far beyond her imagination!

Be steadfast, immovable, always abounding in the work of the Lord, knowing that your toil is not in vain in the Lord.

I Corinthians 15:58 NASB

A good laugh is sunshine in a house.

$\mathcal{P}$eggy was nervous about the upcoming dinner party she and husband were about to host. It was their first time to have guests for dinner since the birth of their son, Pete. To top off Peggy's tension, the guests included her husband Bill's new supervisor.

Sensing the tension in his parents, the baby became irritable and fussy, which only added to Peggy's frustration. In an attempt to comfort little Pete, Peggy picked him up, raised him high over her head, and kissed his bare tummy. To her surprise, he smiled and giggled—the first genuine laugh she had heard from her young son.

In an instant, the evening took on an entirely new tenor. Peggy became more relaxed, and Baby Pete relaxed as well. The dinner party was a great success.

Can the laughter of a little child change a day? Yes! So can the laughter shared between two adults, or the chuckle prompted by the memory of a funny event.

When you're feeling stressed out, don't allow yourself to explode in anger. Get alone if you have to; but find a reason to laugh, and watch the stress melt away!

The light in the eyes [of him whose heart is joyful] rejoices the heart of others.

PROVERBS 15:30 AMP

Each loving act says loud and clear, "I love you. God loves you. I care. God cares."

A warm-from-the-oven casserole taken to the home of a sick friend...

A bouquet of flowers from your garden given to a neighbor...

A thank-you note sent to the performers who did such an excellent job during a concert or play you attended...

A loaf of freshly baked cinnamon bread brought to the office for coffee break...

A box of cookies taken to the police station on Christmas day to encourage those who are on duty during the holiday...

A call to ask with genuine care and concern, "How are you doing?"...

We may not think of these as acts of Christian witnessing, yet they are. Every act of lovingkindness reflects God's lovingkindness for His people. We give because Jesus Christ has so freely given His love to us. He is the example we follow.

Never dismiss an act of lovingkindness as being too small or inconsequential. God will magnify even our smallest deeds to reveal His love to others.

Beloved, let us love one another: for love is of God; and every one that loveth is born of God . . . for God is love.

1 JOHN 4:7,8

I have held many things in my hands and lost them all; but the things I have placed in God's hands, those I always possess.

*T*wo sisters had held a desire from childhood to, one day, go to the mission field together. As they approached mid-life, they realized they were both well established in their professions, and they began to investigate where they might go to serve God. After several months of talking to various missionary agencies, one of the sisters quit her job and moved to South America, where she became involved in pioneering churches.

The other sister, however, decided the hazards of the mission field were too great. She would remain at home and make even more money. "I'll go later," she said as she bid her sister good-bye.

Two years later she died in an accident on the job. She had "saved" her life, only to lose it.

Safety is an illusion apart from God. Many people trust in their jobs—unaware that their companies are on the brink of bankruptcy. Others trust in the government—unaware that funds are diminishing and laws are subject to change. Still others trust in their own abilities, never counting on accidents or illness.

If the Lord has spoken to your heart to "Go," be swift to respond when He opens the door for you to do so.

For I know whom I have believed, and am persuaded that he is able to keep that which I have committed unto him against that day.

2 TIMOTHY 1:12

*A good deed is never lost;
he who sows courtesy reaps
friendship, and he who
plants kindness gathers love.*

Joy Sprague knows how to brighten the days of her customers. As the postmaster for Little Cranberry Island, Maine, she actually has customers competing to get their pictures on her post-office wall. Every twenty-fifth customer to use the U.S. Postal Service's Express Mail has a "mug shot" taken and hung on the wall of the post office—which is actually a portion of the general store—and then is given a plate Joy's home-baked cream puffs!

That's not all Joy does to make Little Cranberry, population ninety, a friendlier place. She operates a mail-order stamp business that is so popular her tiny post office ranks fourth in sales out of 450 outlets in Maine. Why? Most of

Joy's customers are summer visitors who want to stay in contact with the island. Joy sends a snapshot of an island scene and a handwritten note about island events along with each order.

One of the residents has said, "She invents ways to bring pleasure to others." Joy has received praise from the U.S. Postmaster General and has the warm affection not only of the local residents, but friends across America who delight in corresponding with her.

Why not ask the Lord to give you creative ideas which will brighten someone's life today. Perhaps a brief telephone call or post card will remind them how important they really are to you and to God, their Heavenly Father.

Whatsoever a man soweth, that shall he also reap . . . And let us not be weary in well doing: for in due season we shall reap, if we faint not.

GALATIANS 6:7,9

*Kind words can be short
and easy to speak, but
their echoes are truly endless.*

*M*any years ago a famous singer was contracted to perform at a Paris opera house. The event was sold out in a matter of days. The entire city was abuzz with anticipation. That night the hall was packed with stately dressed men and women eager to hear the much-admired musician. The house manager took the stage and announced, "Ladies and gentlemen, thank you for your enthusiastic support. I am afraid that, due to illness, the woman whom you've all come to hear will not be performing tonight. However, we have found a suitable substitute we hope will provide you with comparable entertainment."

The crowd groaned so loudly in its disappointment that few heard the singer's name. Frustration replaced excitement in the hall. The stand-in singer gave everything she had, but when her performance was over she was met with an uncomfortable silence rather than applause. Then, from the balcony, a child stood up and shouted, "Mommy, I think you are wonderful!"

The crowd immediately responded with a thunderous ovation.

Once in a while we each need to hear somebody say, "I think you are wonderful." Why not be the person who gives that kind word of encouragement today!

She opens her mouth in skillful and godly Wisdom, and on her tongue is the law of kindness [giving counsel and instruction.]

PROVERBS 31:26 AMP

*Nothing beats love at first sight
except love with insight.*

Two lifelong friends in their early fifties began to argue over the forthcoming marriage of one of them to a man who was only in his thirties.

"I just don't believe in May-December marriages," the friend said. "After all, December is going to find in May the strength and virility of springtime, but whatever is May going to find in December?"

The bride-to-be thought for a moment and then replied with a twinkle in her eye, "Christmas."

Many couples who claim they "fell in love at first sight" look back after years of marriage and adjust their opinions, saying, "I was infatuated," or "We felt an immediate attraction," or "There was electricity between us when we first met." Love, however, is a word they have come to cherish—it is something they now share that is far richer and meaningful than the emotions they felt "at first sight."

One of the great qualities about genuine love is that it grows and deepens over time. Time is life's nursery for love. Tend to it as you would your most cherished plant, and love's fragrance will continually remain.

The beginning of wisdom is this:
Get wisdom and whatever
else you get, get insight.

PROVERBS 4:7 NRSV

A house is made of walls
and beams; a home is
made of love and dreams.

In *Little House in the Ozarks,* Laura Ingalls Wilder writes, "I spent an afternoon a short time ago with a friend in her new home. The house was beautiful and well-furnished with new furniture, but it seemed bare and empty to me. I wondered why this was until I remembered my experience with my new house. I could not make the living room seem homelike. I would move the chairs here and there and change the pictures on the wall, but something was lacking. Nothing seemed to change the feeling of coldness and vacancy that displeased me whenever I entered the room.

"Then, as I stood in the middle of the room one day wondering what I could possibly do to improve it, it came to me that all that was needed was for someone to live in it and furnish it with the everyday, pleasant thoughts of friendship and cheerfulness and hospitality."[6]

A homey atmosphere is not a matter of the right decorations; it emanates from the thoughts and feelings of the people who live there. Feelings of warmth and welcome can be created only by people who are kind, generous, and even-tempered. Why not determine to "warm-up" the atmosphere where you live today?

Better a meal of vegetables
where there is love than
a fattened calf with hatred.

PROVERBS 15:17 NIV

*The best way to
hold a man
is in your arms.*

*T*his old childhood rhyme is one that many
people remember:

Kiss and hug,
Kiss and hug,
Kiss your sweety
On the mug.

While the rhyme was one children would use
in ridiculing the puppy-love behavior of their
older brothers and sisters, the practice of kissing
and hugging actually has many healthful benefits
beyond those of building a loving relationship.

A West German magazine reported the
results of a study conducted by a life insurance
company. The researchers discovered that husbands who kiss their wives every morning:

live an average of five years longer,

are involved in fewer automobile accidents,
are ill 50 percent less, as noted by sick days,
   and
earn 20 to 30 percent more money.

Other researchers have found that kissing and
hugging releases endorphins, giving mind and
body a sense of genuine well-being that is trans-
lated into better health.

A kiss a day just may keep the doctor away!

*The man should give his wife
all that is her right as a married
woman, and the wife should
do the same for her husband.*

I CORINTHIANS 7:3 TLB

*Ninety percent of the friction
of daily life is caused
by the wrong tone of voice.*

$\mathcal{A}$ demanding wife continually nagged her husband to conform to her very high standards: "This is how you should act, this is how you should dress, this is what you should say, this is where you should be seen, and this is how you should plan your career!" She insisted every aspect of his life be honed to perfection. Feeling thoroughly whipped, the man finally said, "Why don't you just write it all down? Then you won't have to tell me these things all the time." She gladly complied.

A short time later the wife died. Within the course of a year, the man met another woman and married. His new life seemed to be a perpetual honeymoon. He could hardly believe the great joy, and relief, he was experiencing with his new bride.

One day he came across the list of "do's and don'ts" his first wife had written. He read them and realized, to his amazement, he was following all of the instructions—even though his second wife had never mentioned them.

He thought about what might have happened and finally said to a friend, "my former wife began her statements, 'I hate it when . . . ,' but my new wife says, 'I just love it when . . . '"

*A man finds joy in giving
an apt reply—and how
good is a timely word!*

PROVERBS 15:23 NIV

• 57 •

*Forgiveness is giving
love when
there is no reason to.*

*L*isa was shocked when she discovered that David had run up thousands of dollars on every one of their credit cards. Not only was she furious about the mountain of debt, she was frustrated with herself for not recognizing David's habit of compulsive spending.

In the days that followed she wondered if she could ever trust her husband again, and whether they would ever be able to get out of debt.

Rather than wait for something to happen, she took two bold steps. The first was to convince David he needed help, and the second was to seek out a financial planner. She learned if she carefully monitored family funds, they could be out of debt in a few years. This brought hope for the financial future of their marriage.

Another turnaround in their marriage came when David asked Lisa to forgive him. She found that forgiving David freed her to turn away from the matter of money and to focus on their relationship. She decided it was possible to love someone even though they had "messed up." Forgiving made trust possible again, and once trust was reestablished their marriage began to be healed.

Forgiveness turns the heart away from what was and is, to what can be. Is it time for you to take some bold steps? If love is your motive, be encouraged. Situations can change.

"Blessed are the merciful,
for they shall obtain mercy."

MATTHEW 5:7 NKJV

*Nothing is so strong
as gentleness. Nothing is
so gentle as real strength.*

Mentor Graham was so absorbed in evaluating assignments, he failed to notice the youthful giant who slouched into his Illinois schoolroom one day after school. After his eyes had adjusted to the brightness of the late-afternoon sunshine, causing the husky young man to be in silhouette before him, he recognized the youth as a newcomer to the community. The lad already had a reputation for "whipping the daylights" out of all the local toughs.

Graham would have been justified in thinking, *What does he want here? Am I in danger?* Rather, he looked up and down the six-foot-four-inches of muscle and ignorance before him and offered to help the lad with his reading. When the young man left the schoolroom an hour later, he had several books under his arm—a loan from Mentor Graham with a promise of more in the future.

Few people remember Graham. He was a quiet man, simply willing to do his best for any student who came his way. His pupil, however, became far more famous. His name was Abraham Lincoln.

A kind, helpful response to others is often perceived by them as strength. It is this gentle strength to which we are drawn. When you think you find yourself in a touchy situation, try a gentle touch!

Thou hast also given me the shield of Thy salvation, and Thy right hand upholds me; and Thy gentleness makes me great.

PSALM 18:35 NASB

Everyone has patience.
Successful people learn to use it.

Several years ago a speedboat driver was in
a serious accident. In recounting what had happened, she said that she had been at top speed
when her boat veered just slightly, hitting a wave
at a dangerous angle. The combined force of her
speed and the size and angle of the wave sent the
boat spinning wildly into the air. She was thrown
from her seat and propelled deeply into the
water. She was thrust so deeply into the water
that she could not see any light from the surface.
Being a little dazed, she had no idea which direction was up.

Rather than panic, the woman remained calm
and waited for the buoyancy of her life vest to
begin pulling her up. Then she swam heartily in
that direction.

We often find ourselves surrounded by many voices, each with a different opinion, and we simply don't know which way is up. When this happens we need to exercise patience and spend time with the Lord. We must read His Word, the Bible, and wait for His gentle tug on our hearts to pull us toward His will. The more we read, the more confident we will become, especially when His written Word and that gentle tug on our hearts come into agreement.

Remember, a few minutes, hours, days, or even months of "waiting" may mean the difference between sinking or floating.

Let patience have her perfect work,
that ye may be perfect and entire,
wanting nothing.

JAMES 1:4

*Watch out for temptation—
the more you see of it
the better it looks.*

*A*s a teen, Megan arrived home from school just in time to watch an hour of "soap operas" before doing her homework. She enjoyed the escape into the TV world and wasn't really aware that the programs were creating an inordinate amount of sexual curiosity in her. Over months and even years of watching her two "soaps," Megan's perspective on life took a shift. She began to think, *Relationships don't need to be pure—in fact, the impure ones seem more exciting. Fidelity doesn't matter, as long as a person is happy.*

As a college student, Megan found it easy to participate in "one-night stands." Then, after a short marriage ended in catastrophe as a result of her infidelity, she sought help from a counselor.

At the outset, it was difficult for the counselor to understand why Megan had engaged in extramarital affairs. She had been a model teenager at home, church, and school as far as her public behavior was concerned. Finally, the counselor discovered the source of the temptations that drove Megan to participate in her supposed hidden life.

What we see on TV inevitably becomes a part of our memory bank, becoming background information for "justified" behavior. If what you see isn't what you want to do, then change what you see.

Keep watching and praying, that you may not come into temptation.

MARK 14:38 NASB

It is such a comfort to drop the tangles of life into God's hands and leave them there.

Many years ago, a young woman who felt called to the ministry was accepted into a noted seminary. There were only two other women enrolled, and her very presence seemed to make her male classmates uncomfortable. She felt isolated, yet on display at the same time. To make matters worse, many of her professors were doing their best to destroy her faith rather than build it up. Even her private time of devotions seemed dry and lonely.

At Christmas break she sought her father's counsel. "How can I be strong in my resolve and straight in my theology with all that I face there?"

Her father took a pencil from his pocket and laid it on the palm of his hand. "Can that pencil stand upright by itself?" he asked her.

"No," she replied. Then her father grasped the pencil in his hand and held it in an upright position. "Ah," she said, "but your are holding it now."

"Daughter," he replied, "your life is like this pencil. But Jesus Christ is the one who can hold you." The young woman took her pencil and returned to seminary.

*Cast your cares on the Lord
and he will sustain you.*

PSALM 55:22 NIV

Friendship improves happiness, and abates misery, by doubling our joy, and dividing our grief.

They call themselves the "Ladies of the Lake," but they never set out to be a club. Rather, the group began when one of the women returned home exhausted from a business trip and came to the conclusion that she had too much of one thing in her life: MEN! With a husband and two boys at home, a work environment that was mostly male, and an elderly father and uncle for which to care, she resolved to set some time aside for herself and a few female friends.

Over the years, Paula hadn't cultivated very many friendships with other women, but she was determined to see that change. Eventually she discovered three like-minded women: one owned a machine shop, one worked for a contractor, and one ran a truck stop. The women pulled out their calendars over dinner one evening and agreed on this schedule—"A trip to the lake at least once a quarter!"

At the lake, the women would listen to Mozart, fix gourmet dinners, and sit on the deck overlooking the water. They would talk for hours—about everything—without an agenda.

Over the years, they became very close and often refer to each other as "sister." Says Paula, "Nobody understands like another woman."

A friend loves at all times, and
a brother is born for adversity.

PROVERBS 17:17 NIV

Everyone has an invisible sign
hanging from his neck saying,
"Make me feel important!"

It Isn't Enough

It isn't enough to say in our hearts
That we like a man for his ways,
It isn't enough that we fill our minds
With paeans of silent praise;
Nor is it enough that we honor a man
As our confidence upward mounts,
It's going right up to the man himself,
And telling him so that counts!
If a man does a work you really admire,
Don't leave a kind word unsaid,
In fear that to do so might make him vain
And cause him to "lose his head."
But reach out your hand and tell him,
"Well done," and see how his gratitude swells;
It isn't the flowers wc strew on the grave,
It's the word to the living that tells.

                                        Anonymous

For lack of praise, many think others draw negative conclusions about them. We can actually wound people by withholding our praise. Let someone know you think well of him or her today. What a difference your words will make!

Therefore encourage one another and build each other up, just as in fact you are doing.

I Thessalonians 5:11 niv

You cannot do a kindness too soon, because you never know how soon it will be too late!

William McKinley served in Congress before he was elected the twenty-fifth President of the United States. On his way to his congressional office one morning, he boarded a streetcar and took the only remaining seat. Minutes later, a woman who appeared to be ill boarded the car. Unable to find a seat, she clutched an overhead strap next to one of McKinley's colleagues. The other congressman hid behind his newspaper and did not offer the woman his seat. McKinley walked up the aisle, tapped the woman on the shoulder, offered her his seat, and took her place in the aisle.

Years later when McKinley was President, this same congressman was recommended to him for a post as ambassador to a foreign nation.

McKinley refused to appoint him. He feared a man who didn't have the courtesy to offer his seat to a sick woman in a crowded streetcar would lack the courtesy and sensitivity necessary to be an ambassador in a troubled nation. The disappointed congressman bemoaned his fate to many in Washington, but never did learn why McKinley chose someone else for the position.

Acts of kindness can lead you to prominence. Then, from that position of prominence, you can be kind to even more people.

*Encourage one another day after day,
as long as it is still called "Today."*

HEBREWS 3:13 NASB

Stack every bit of criticism between two layers of praise.

Shortly after graduation, Joe and Lana married. One of their first marital discoveries was their very different understanding of "being on time." Not wanting to end the honeymoon stage too early, Lana found herself mildly complaining about Joe's being late. But Joe never took the hint, and soon her complaining turned to outright criticism.

On the surface, there may not seem to be much difference between exposing a problem and criticizing, but in a relationship, the choice of words can bring very different responses. Criticism attacks someone's personality and character. When Lana *criticized* Joe, she would say, "You're only thinking about yourself!"

Putting an issue on the table for discussion in a positive manner is the first step toward finding a resolution. A person who asks gently, "Does it embarrass you when we are late?" is opening a dialog for finding the solution to the problem. Criticism only wounds the spirit, puts the other person on the defensive, and usually ends up in a no-resolution argument.

Watch what you say! Criticism can cause a wound that takes years to heal, but a kind and gracious attitude in problem-solving can save you years of tears.

Correct, rebuke and encourage—with great patience and careful instruction.

2 TIMOTHY 4:2 NIV

In trying times,
don't quit trying.

Somebody said that it couldn't be done,
But he with a chuckle replied,
That "maybe it couldn't" but he would be one
Who wouldn't say so till he'd tried.
So he buckled right in with the trace of a grin
On his face. If he worried, he hid it.
He started to sing as he tackled the thing
That couldn't be done. And he did it.
Somebody scoffed: "Oh, you'll never do that,
At least no one ever has done it."
But he took off his coat and took off his hat
And the first thing he knew he'd begun it.
With the lift of his chin and a bit of a grin,
If any doubt rose he forbid it;
He started to sing as he tackled the thing
That couldn't be done, and he did it.
There are thousands to tell you it cannot
be done,

There are thousands to prophesy failure;
There are thousands to point out to you, one
   by one,
The dangers that wait to assail you,
But just buckle right in with a bit of a grin,
Then take off your coat and go to it.
Just start in to sing as you tackle the thing
That cannot be done, and you'll do it.

                            —Edgar A. Guest

Let us not be weary in
well doing, for in due season
we shall reap, if we faint not.

GALATIANS 6:9

To love what you do and feel that it matters—how could anything be more fun?

 A newspaper in England once asked this question of its readers, "Who are the happiest people on the earth?"

The four prize-winning answers were:

A little child building sand castles.

A craftsman or artist whistling over a job well done.

A mother, bathing her baby after a busy day.

A doctor who has finished a difficult and dangerous operation that saved a human life.

The paper's editors were surprised to find virtually no one submitted kings, emperors, millionaires, or others of riches and rank as the happiest people on earth.

W. Beran Wolfe once said, "If you observe a really happy man you will find him building a boat, writing a symphony, educating his son, growing double dahlias in his garden, or looking for dinosaur eggs in the Gobi desert. He will not be searching for happiness as if it were a collar button that has rolled under the radiator. He will not be striving for it as a goal in itself. He will have become aware that he is happy in the course of living life twenty-four crowded hours of the day."

When you eat the labor of
your hands, you shall be happy,
and it shall be well with you.

PSALM 128:2 NKJV

*Life is a coin. You can spend
it any way you wish, but
you can only spend it once.*

*A*nita Septimus has worked as a social
worker for HIV-infected children since 1985. In
the first few months she worked with her tiny
clients, three of them died. Despair began to
overwhelm her. She made a commitment to stick
with the job for three more months, during
which time she could not get a friend's words
out of her thoughts, "You have not chosen a
pretty profession."

She had to admit, her friend was right. It
took resolve to accept that fact and simply do
what she could to help families make the most of
what remained of their children's lives. She is
still there.

Over the last ten years, her clinic has grown
considerably. Today, Anita and her staff care for

more than three hundred families with AIDS children. They go into their homes, teach infection prevention, and help the parents plan for the future. The children are regularly taken on trips to the zoo, the circus, and summer camps.

One AIDS baby wasn't expected to see her first birthday, but she recently celebrated her tenth. Such "long-term" clients give back to Anita what she terms "an indestructible sense of hope"—a precious gift!

What is your life? It is even a vapour,
that appeareth for a little time,
and then vanisheth away.

JAMES 4:14

Diligence is the mother of good fortune.

*O*n a shelf sits a beautiful and expensive carving from the Orient. It is a statue of a lady wearing a tall headdress, and balanced atop the headdress is an intricately carved ball. Inside that seamless sphere is another slightly smaller sphere of equal intricacy—and inside that still another, and then another—until one can no longer see through the tiny carved holes to see how many more balls there actually are.

Several things make this orb truly remarkable. Each of the nested balls is seamless, completely free from the one outside it and inside it, and magnificent in its airy, lacy design. The orb was carved from a single piece of ivory over one hundred years ago, before the days of electronic magnifying instruments.

Why did the artist carve so many layers with such precision? The smallest orbs would not be clearly seen by most people, yet each one was finished with as much skill and artistry as was applied to the larger, outer ones.

The small details of a job may not always remain unnoticed or unseen. Like this artist, your excellence in small things can bring you prosperity in this life and make you a legend for future generations to follow.

The hand of the diligent
makes one rich.

PROVERBS 10:4 NKJV

*The most wasted of all
days is that on which
one has not laughed.*

A little girl was eating her breakfast one
morning when a ray of sunlight suddenly
appeared through the clouds and reflected off
the spoon in her cereal bowl. She immediately
put it into her mouth. With a big smile she
exclaimed to her mother, "I just swallowed a
spoonful of sunshine!"

A spoonful of sunshine just may be the best
"soul food" that a person can have in a day. A
prominent surgeon once wrote, "Encourage your
child to be merry and to laugh aloud. A good,
hearty laugh expands the chest and makes the
blood bound merrily along. A good laugh will
sound right through the house. It will not only do
your child good, but will be a benefit to all who
hear, and be an important means of driving the

blues away from a dwelling. Merriment is very catching, and spreads in a remarkable manner, few being able to resist the contagion. A hearty laugh is delightful harmony; indeed it is the best of music."

An old poem advises: If you are on the gloomy line, the worry train, or the grouchy track, get a transfer! It's time to climb aboard the sunshine train and sit in one of its cheerful cars.

A happy heart makes the face cheerful, but heartache crushes the spirit.

PROVERBS 15:13 NIV

You can accomplish more in one hour with God than one lifetime without Him.

In *A Closer Walk,* Catherine Marshall writes about a neighbor, "Cynthia felt she was losing her identity in an endless procession of social events and chauffeuring of children. During one cocktail party, Cynthia decided to limit herself to ginger ale and made some discoveries—not especially pleasant: 'I saw our crowd through new eyes', she told me. 'No one was really saying anything. . . . All at once I began to ask questions about what we call "the good life."'

"In a search for answers, Cynthia set aside an hour each day for meditation. As she did this over a period of weeks there came to her the realization that she was being met in this quiet hour by something more than her own thoughts and psyche. . . . By Someone who loved her and insisted this love be passed on to her family and friends."

Cynthia made changes in her life as the result of her "hour with God." She turned meal times into a time for family sharing. Family Game Night became a substitute for television once a week. She and her husband joined a Bible study that met twice a month. In all, Cynthia concluded, "God. . . . the Author of creativity, is ready to make a dull life adventuresome the moment we allow His Holy Spirit to go to work."[7]

Walk in wisdom . . .
redeeming the time.

COLOSSIANS 4:5

*Courage is resistance
to fear, mastery of fear.
Not the absence of fear.*

Napoleon called Marshall Ney the bravest man he had ever known. Yet Ney's knees trembled so badly one morning before a battle, he had difficulty mounting his horse. When he finally was in the saddle, he shouted contemptuously down at his limbs, "Shake away, knees. You would shake worse than that if you knew where I am going to take you."

Courage is not a matter of not being afraid. It is a matter of taking action even when you are afraid.

Courage is also more than sheer bravado—shouting, "I can do this!" and launching out with a do-or-die attitude over some reckless dare.

True courage is manifest when a person chooses to take a difficult or even dangerous course of action because it is the right thing to do. Courage is looking beyond yourself to what is best for another.

The source of all courage is the Holy Spirit of God, our Comforter. It is His nature to remain by our side to help us. When we welcome Him into our lives and He compels us to do something, we can confidently trust He will be right there, helping us get it done.

Therefore, take up the full armor of God, that you may be able to resist in the evil day, and having done everything, to stand firm. Stand firm therefore.

Ephesians 6:13-14 NASB

The art of being wise is the art of knowing what to overlook.

 The story is told of a couple at their golden wedding anniversary celebration. Surrounded by her children, grandchildren, and great grandchildren, the wife was asked the secret to a long and happy marriage. With a loving glance toward her husband, she answered: "On my wedding day, I decided to make a list of ten of my husband's faults which, for the sake of our marriage, I would overlook. I figured I could live with at least ten faults."

 A guest asked her to identify some of the faults she had chosen to overlook. Her husband looked a bit troubled at the thought of having his foibles and flaws revealed to the assembled group. However, his wife sweetly replied, "To tell you the truth, dear, I never did get around to listing them. Instead, every time my husband did something that made me hopping mad, I would simply say to myself, *Lucky for him that's one of the ten!*"

Even the most devoted friends and spouses will experience storms in their relationships from time to time. Some problems are worth addressing in order to resolve them. Others are best left undiscussed. In time, issues of little importance tend to blow past without any need for "blowup."

A man's wisdom gives him patience;
it is to his glory to overlook an offense.

PROVERBS 19:11 NIV

• 91 •

*Triumph is just "umph"
added to try.*

*M*onica Seles recently won her first tennis tournament in more than two years since she had been stabbed in the shoulder by a crazed fan.

Withstanding one hundred-degree heat and tendinitis in her left knee, she roared through the Canadian Open to defeat three Top 20 players en route to a finals match that lasted only fifty-one minutes. Her nightmare recovery had truly come to an end.

To help in her recovery, Monica asked Olympic champion Jackie Joyner-Kersee and her coach/husband, Bob Kersee, to put her on a strict workout routine. While on this physical regimen she also worked to overcome the emotional problems that accompany such an attack.

Her father and coach, Karolj, who had been stricken by prostate and stomach cancer, was her continual source of inspiration. She said, "I was down and he came into my room and said he couldn't stand to see me that way. I decided then that I had to try and put it behind me and move on."

Have you ever felt "stabbed in the back" while doing good? Withdrawal is often our first temptation, but with a creative and loving God, who continually inspires us, we just can't quit! Our detractors will have to say about us what was said about Monica, "She's back!"

Let us not be weary in
well-doing: for in due season
we shall reap, if we faint not.

GALATIANS 6:9

*People don't care how much
you know, until they know how
much you care . . . about them.*

*O*n a bitter, cold Virginia evening, an old
man waited on a path by a river, hoping for
someone on a horse to carry him across. His
beard was glazed with frost, and his body grew
numb before he finally heard the thunder of
horses' hooves. Anxiously he watched as several
horsemen appeared. He let the first pass by
without making an effort to get his attention,
then another and another. Finally, only one rider
remained. As he drew near, the old man caught
his eye and asked, "Sir, would you mind giving
me a ride to the other side?"

The rider helped the man onto this horse
and, sensing he was half-frozen, decided to take
him all the way home, which was several miles
out of the way. As they rode, the horseman asked,

"Why didn't you ask one of the other men to help you? I was the last one. What if I had refused?"

The old man said, "I've been around a while, son, and I know people pretty well. When I looked into their eyes and saw they had no concern for my condition, I knew it was useless to ask. When I looked into your eyes, I saw kindness and compassion."

At the door of the old man's house the rider resolved, "May I never get too busy in my own affairs that I fail to respond to the needs of others." And with that, Thomas Jefferson turned and directed his horse back to the White House.

Though I have the gift of prophecy,
and understand all mysteries, and all
knowledge; and though I have all faith,
so that I could remove mountains,
and have not charity, I am nothing.

1 CORINTHIANS 13:2

Good words are worth much, and cost little.

*I*t takes just as much energy to say a positive word as it does a negative one. In fact, it may take even less. Research has shown that when we speak positive words—even in difficult circumstances or troubling situations—our bodies relax. As we relax, blood flow increases, including the flow of blood to the brain. A well-oxygenated brain is much more likely to think creatively, make wise decisions, find reasonable solutions, and generate answers to questions.

Positive words ease relationships and create an atmosphere of peace that is conducive to rest, relaxation, rejuvenation, and sleep—all of which are necessary for good health.

On the other hand, contrary to popular thought, negative words do not release tension. They keep the body in a state of tension, constricting muscles and blood vessels. Irrational, uncreative, unreasonable behavior is a secondary effect.

A continual flow of negative words causes relationships to suffer, which creates an atmosphere of disharmony and makes for fitful sleep and frayed nerves—none of which are healthy.

One of the best things we can do for our overall health is to transform our speech habits.

Pleasant words are a honeycomb, sweet to the soul and healing to the bones.

PROVERBS 16:24 NASB

• 97 •

*I don't know the secret to
success, but the key to failure
is to try to please everyone.*

The story is told of a painter who desired
to produce one work which would please the
entire world. She drew a picture which required
her utmost skill and took it to the public market-
place. She posted directions at the bottom of the
piece for spectators to mark with a brush each
portion of the picture that didn't meet their
approval. The spectators came and, in general,
applauded the work. But each, eager to make a
personal critique, marked a small portion of the
picture. By evening, the painter was mortified to
find the entire picture had become a blot.

The next day the painter returned with a
copy of the first picture. This time she asked the
spectators to mark the portions of the work they
admired. The spectators again complied. When

the artist returned several hours later, she found every stroke that had been panned the day before had received praise by this day's critics.

The artist concluded, "I now believe the best way to please one-half of the world is not to mind what the other says."

People will always have an opinion about what we say or do. That is why we live our lives according to the words of the Bible—God's opinion. Then we will not fret over the opinions of others.

"No one can serve two masters;
for either he will hate the one
and love the other, or he will hold
to one and despise the other."

MATTHEW 6:24 NASB

• 99 •

No one is useless in this world who lightens the burden of it to anyone else.

 *C*arol Porter, a registered nurse, is a co-founder of Kid-Care, Inc., a nonprofit group with a volunteer staff who deliver five hundred free meals each day to poor neighborhoods. Each meal is prepared in Porter's cramped Houston home, where extra stoves and refrigerators have been installed in what used to be the family's living room and den. Kid-Care receives no public funding, and although Carol's efforts have resulted in help from some corporations, most of her $500,000 budget comes from individual donations.

Carol credits her late mother, Lula Doe, for giving her the idea for Kid-Care. In 1984 Lula persuaded a local supermarket not to discard its blemished produce, but to let her distribute it to the poor.

During Christmas time in 1989, Carol saw a group of children searching for food in a McDonalds' dumpster. She says, "I saw Third World conditions a stone's throw from where I live." Kid-Care was her response.

"People ask me what's in it for me. And I tell them to go the route with me and see my kids' faces. That's what's in it for me." She sees the meals as "better than ice cream. . . . It's hope."[8]

Purpose in life comes when we purpose to lift the load of another—to show God's love by doing for them what they could not do for themselves.

Bear ye one another's burdens,
and so fulfill the law of Christ.

GALATIANS 6:2

Do not follow where the path may lead—go instead where there is no path and leave a trail.

Many years ago an intern in a New York hospital heard a surgeon bemoan the fact that most brain tumors were fatal. The surgeon predicted some day a surgeon would discover how to save the lives of these patients. Intern Ernest Sachs dared to be that surgeon. At the time, the leading expert on the anatomy of the brain was Sir Victor Horsley. Sachs received permission to study under him, but felt he should prepare for the experience by studying for six months under some of the most able physicians in Germany. Then he went to England, where for two years he assisted Dr. Horsley in long and intricate experiments on dozens of monkeys.

When Sachs returned to America he was ridiculed for requesting the opportunity to treat brain tumors. For years he fought obstacles and discouragement, driven by an uncontrollable urge to succeed in his quest. Today, largely thanks to Dr. Sachs, the majority of brain tumors can be cured. His book, *The Diagnosis and Treatment of Brain Tumors,* is considered the standard authority on the subject.

Because something isn't presently done doesn't mean it *can't* be done. And maybe you are the one to do it!

Your ears shall hear a word
behind you, saying,
"This is the way, walk in it."

ISAIAH 30:21 NKJV

*There is one thing alone that
stands the brunt of life
throughout its length;
a quiet conscience.*

*P*resident Woodrow Wilson was
approached one day by one of his secretaries,
who suggested he take off from his work to enjoy
a particular diversion he enjoyed. President
Wilson replied, "My boss won't let me do it."

"Your boss?" the secretary asked, wondering
who could be the boss of the chief executive of
the United States.

"Yes," said Wilson. "I have a conscience that is
my boss. It drives me to the task, and it will not
let me accept this tempting invitation."

Our conscience is one of the most prized
items we posses. It is through our conscience we
receive inner promptings from God which, when

in agreement with our actions, will point us toward a safe and eternal way.

It has been said, "A conscience is like a thermostat on an air conditioning unit—it kicks in when things are on the verge of getting too hot."

It is possible to ignore our conscience and "follow the crowd," but this is a sad waste of our lives. The conscience is the window to the soul through which we hear the voice of God, Who always leads us to success and inner peace.

Listen carefully, He may have something good to say!

If our hearts do not condemn us,
we have confidence before God.

I JOHN 3:21 NIV

*My obligation is to
do the right thing.
The rest is in God's hands.*

*I*n *Dakota,* Kathleen Norris writes: "A Benedictine sister from the Philippines once told me what her community did when some sisters took to the streets in the popular revolt against Marcos' regime. Some did not think it proper for nuns to demonstrate in public, let alone risk arrest. In a group meeting that began and ended with prayer, the sisters who wished to continue demonstrating explained that this was for them a religious obligation; those who disapproved also had their say. Everyone spoke; everyone heard and gave counsel.

"It was eventually decided that the nuns who were demonstrating should continue to do so; those who wished to express solidarity but were unable to march would prepare food and provide medical assistance to the demonstrators, and those who disapproved would pray for everyone. The sisters laughed and said, If one of the conservative sisters was praying that we young, crazy ones would come to our senses and stay off the streets, that was O.K. We were still a community."[9]

God calls some to action, others to support, and still others to pray. Each will be doing what is right in His eyes if they obey His call.

If you know that he is righteous,
you may be sure that everyone
who does right is born of him.

1 JOHN 2:29 RSV

Expect great things from God.
Attempt great things for God.

Gladys Aylward saw herself as a simple woman who just did what God called her to do. Yet, her life was so remarkable that both a book *(The Small Woman)* and a movie *(The Inn of Sixth Happiness)* were produced about the great things God accomplished through her.

A British citizen, Aylward left her home in 1920 and sailed for China. There she bought orphans who were being systematically discarded, children who had been displaced by the political upheavals of the time and left to starve or wander on their own until placed in government warehouses. Gladys gave these children a home.

When the Japanese invaded China, she was forced to flee the mainland with one hundred children. She ended up on the island of Formosa with her charges. There she continued to devote her life to raising children who knew no other mother.

Gladys explains her amazing work for God like this: "I did not choose this. I was led into it by God. I am not really more interested in children than I am in other people, but God through His Holy Spirit gave me to understand that this is what He wanted me to do, so I did."

"Truly, truly, I say to you,
he who believes in Me, the works
that I do shall he do also; and
greater works than these shall
he do; because I go to the Father."

JOHN 14:12 NASB

Dost thou love life? Then do not squander time, for that is the stuff life is made of.

A woman once had a dream that an angel was giving her this message: "As a reward for your virtues, the sum of $1,440 will be deposited into your bank account every morning. This amount has only one condition. At the close of each business day, any balance that has not been used will be canceled. It won't carry over to the next day or accrue interest. Each morning, a new $1,440 will be credited to you."

The dream was so vivid, she asked the Lord to show her what it meant. He led her to realize she was receiving 1,440 minutes every morning, the total number of minutes in a 24-hour day. What she did with this deposit of time was important, because 1,440 minutes per day was all she would ever receive!

Each of us has a similar account. At the close of each "business" day, we should be able to look over our ledger and see that these golden minutes were spent wisely.

Time is God's gift to you. What you do with your time is your gift to God.

Remember how short my time is.

PSALM 89:47

The grass may be greener
on the other side, but
it still has to be mowed.

Several years ago, a newspaper cartoon was drawn of two fields divided by a fence. Both were about the same size, and each had plenty of lush, green grass.

Each field had a mule whose head stuck through the wire fence, eating grass from the other's pasture. The neighboring field seemed somewhat more desirable—even though it was harder to reach.

In the process, the mules' heads became caught in the fence. They panicked and brayed uncontrollably at being unable to free themselves. The cartoonist wisely described the situation with one caption: "DISCONTENT."

Like the mules, when we focus on what we don't have we become blinded to the blessings which surround us. There is nothing wrong with desiring something, but to think life is easier in someone else's pasture may not be true. Besides, no matter whose pasture we are in, we will always have to deal with the attitudes of our own heart.

If there is something you desire in life, perhaps a home, a better car, or even your own business, look to Jesus to help you bring it to pass. And while He is working on it, remember to find pleasure in what He's already given you!

Be content with such
things as ye have.

HEBREWS 13:5

• 113 •

Every job is a self-portrait of the person who does it. Autograph your work with excellence.

Someone once asked Al Jolson, a popular musical comedy star of the twenties, what he did to warm up a cold audience. Jolson answered, "Whenever I go out before an audience and don't get the response I feel that I ought to get, . . . I don't go back behind the scenes and say to myself, 'That audience is dead from the neck up—it's a bunch of wooden nutmegs.' No, instead I say to myself, 'Look here, Al, what is wrong with you tonight? The audience is all right, but you're all wrong, Al."

Many a performer has blamed a poor showing on an audience. Al Jolson took a different approach. He tried to give the best performance of his career to his coldest, most unresponsive audiences, and the result was that before an evening was over, he had them applauding and begging for more.

You'll always be able to find excuses for mediocrity. In fact, a person intent on justifying a bad performance usually has excuses lined up before the final curtain falls. Choose instead to put your full energy into your performance. Your extra effort will turn an average performance into something outstanding.

Ah, the joys of a job well done. That is true satisfaction!

Many daughters have done well,
But you excel them all.

PROVERBS 31:29 NKJV

The greatest achievements
are those that benefit others.

A recent plot of the soap opera *All My Children* called for high-society philanthropist Brooke English to move into a homeless shelter to better understand their plight. Julia Barr, who plays Brooke, felt prompted by the part to take some real-life action of her own. She became a participant in First Step, a New York City job-readiness program for homeless and formerly homeless women. The eight-week session included one-on-one mentoring, résumé advice, access to job internships, interview clothing, and pep talks from people such as herself.

Says Julia, "I know how it feels to lack motivation and self-esteem. I tend to procrastinate; I'm rarely on time; I'm rather bossy; I'm very stubborn—we all have things that hold us back, and so I share mine."[10]

Julia is not only giving her time but also her money. When her maternal grandmother, Myrtle, died at the age of 104, she left Julia a nice amount of money. It was all donated to First Step.

Julia Barr has one Emmy award and six nominations, but those in First Step will remember her for the care she gave to them.

To be the greatest, be a servant.

MATTHEW 23:11 TLB

If a task is once begun,
never leave it till it's done.
Be the labor great or small,
do it well or not at all.

$\mathcal{A}$ series of illustrations in a popular magazine once depicted the life-story of a "one-note musician." From frame to frame, the tale revealed how the woman followed her daily routine of eating and sleeping until the time came for the evening concert. She carefully inspected her music on the stand and tuned her instrument. As the concert began, the conductor skillfully cued first one group of musicians and then another until finally, the crucial moment arrived. It was time for the one note to be played!

The conductor turned to the violinist and signaled her to sound her note. She did, and then the moment was over. The orchestra played on and the "one-note" woman sat quietly through the rest of the concert—not with a sense of disappointment that she had played only one note, but with a sense of contentment and peace of mind that she had played her one note in tune, on time, and with great gusto.

Sometimes "one-note" people are criticized for being limited or narrow in their perspective by those whose lifestyle requires the wearing of many "hats." But a job well done by others is valued by God, so it certainly deserves our recognition and respect.

Whatever your hand finds to do,
do it with your might.

ECCLESIASTES 9:10 NKJV

• 119 •

*I would rather walk with
God in the dark than
go alone in the light.*

On February 11, 1861, President-elect
Lincoln left his home in Springfield to begin his
rail journey to Washington, where he was to be
inaugurated a month later. Lincoln had a premo-
nition this would be the last time he would see
Springfield. Standing on the rear platform of his
railroad car, he bid the townspeople farewell. He
closed his remarks with these words: "Today I
leave you. I go to assume a task more difficult
than that which devolved upon General
Washington. The great God which guided him
must help me. Without that assistance I shall
surely fail; with it, I cannot fail."

The same is true for us, regardless of the
tasks we face. Without God's assistance, we
cannot succeed. We may get the dishes washed,

the laundry folded, and the beds made. We may get our work done without accident or incident. We may find what we need at the market and manage to keep a schedule. But without God's help, our lives would be a confused mess.

Does God care about what happens in our day? Absolutely! When we become overwhelmed, making the smallest of tasks into mountains, He helps us to gather ourselves. Step-by-step, He shows us the way, and our strength is renewed to go on.

Even when walking through the dark valley of death I will not be afraid, for you are close beside me, guarding, guiding all the way.

PSALM 23:4 TLB

*All our dreams can
come true—if we have the
courage to pursue them.*

Sports psychologists have identified six reoccurring traits common among gold-medallist athletes. These "traits of a champion" apply to both men and women, and are also dominant factors in the lives of those who succeed in non-athletic vocations.

1. *Self-analysis.* These successful athletes know their strengths and weaknesses, and engage in critical appraisal that is honest, but never negative.

2. *Self-competition.* Winners know they can only control their own performances, so they compete against their own best efforts, not that of others.

3. *Focus.* The champion is always "in the present," concentrating on the task at hand.

4. *Confidence.* Successful athletes control anxiety by setting tough but reasonable goals. As goals are reached, confidence increases.

5. *Toughness.* This is a mental trait that involves accepting risk and trying to win, rather than trying not to lose. Winners see change as opportunities and accept responsibility for their own destinies.

6. *Having a game plan.* Even elite athletes know talent is not enough. They have a game plan.[11]

Everyone can develop these traits. *Everyone!*

Be strong and courageous, and act; do not fear nor be dismayed, for the LORD God, my God, is with you.

1 CHRONICLES 28:20 NASB

*Remember the banana—when it
left the bunch, it got skinned.*

*T*he next time you visit a very dense forest,
try to imagine what is taking place under your
feet. Scientists now know when the roots of trees
come into contact with one another, a substance
is released which encourages the growth of a particular kind of fungus. This fungus helps link
roots of different trees—even those of dissimilar
species. If one tree has access to water, another to
nutrients, and a third to sunlight, the fungus
enables the transfer of these items to trees that
may be in need. Thus the trees have the means of
sharing with one another to preserve them all.

Our culture today applauds individualism.
This isolates people from one another and cuts
them off from the mainstream of life. With more
and more people working at home or in walled
offices, and with schedules crammed tighter than

ever with work and activities, feelings of loneliness are more likely to increase than decrease. Don't allow isolation to overcome you!

Reach out to others. Begin to give where you can. Learn to receive when others give to you. Build a network of friends, not just colleagues. And above all, root yourself in a group that nourishes you spiritually—a church.

Not forsaking the assembling of ourselves together, as the manner of some is; but exhorting one another; and so much the more, as ye see the day approaching.

HEBREWS 10:25

Decisions can take you out of God's will but never out of His reach.

When Cathy met Jim at a softball game, she thought he was the man for her—everything she was looking for! After several months of dating, Cathy was as sold on Jim as ever, except it bothered her that he found so many excuses for drinking alcohol. "I got a raise!" "My friend is getting married!" "My sister is graduating from college!"

Despite her friends' warnings and her own misgivings, Cathy married Jim. Before long, however, the marriage was destroyed by Jim's drinking. When the divorce was final, Cathy felt destroyed too. By ignoring the Holy Spirit's warning and her friends' wise counsel, she had made one of the biggest mistakes a Christian could make. I wanted to have my way instead of

God's," Cathy told her pastor. "I thought I knew what was best for me."

"We all think that sometimes," Cathy's pastor said. "We forget that the One who created us knows us better than we know ourselves. But remember, Cathy, He never gives up on us! When we admit our mistakes, He always forgives us and gives us another chance."

Recovering from the bad choices we've made can be heart-wrenching and difficult, but God is always right there ready to make us whole and give us a brand new life.

If we are faithless, he will remain faithful, for he cannot disown himself.

2 TIMOTHY 2:13 NIV

"No" is one of the few words that can never be misunderstood.

While in medical training, surgeons are encouraged to weigh the importance of each word spoken during an operation. As the anesthetic is given, fear may strike a patient if she hears someone say, "I'm going to shoot her now." Even a phrase such as "hook up the monitor" may be interpreted by a drugged patient as sounding like "shake up the monster." Can you imagine the impact on a half-dazed patient if she hears a doctor say, "This isn't my day!"

The same directions given by two different physicians could encourage or discourage a patient, simply by their tone of voice. One doctor's voice might suggest a prescription will work, while another's voice might convey reservations. Either would drastically affect the morale of a patient.

Theodore Roosevelt popularized an expression about the need for clear, precise communication. He called words with several possible meanings "weasel words"—by using them a speaker might weasel out of any commitment, claiming a different interpretation of the word.

The Bible also tells us again and again to remember the importance of our words. We are always to speak words of encouragement, hope, and faith to those around us.

*"Let your statement be
'Yes, yes' or 'No, no.'"*

MATTHEW 5:37 NASB

• 129 •

Some people complain because God put thorns on roses, while others praise Him for putting roses among thorns.

One rainy day a woman overheard someone say, "What miserable weather!" She looked out her office window to see a big, fat robin using a nearby puddle of water for a bathtub. He was splashing and fluttering, thoroughly enjoying himself. She couldn't help but think, *Miserable for whom? It's all a matter of perspective.*

That's a lesson that Lincoln Steffens learned as a young boy. He was watching an artist paint a picture of a muddy river. He told the artist he didn't like the picture because there was so much mud in it. The artist admitted there was mud in the picture, but what he saw was the beautiful colors and contrasts of the light against the dark.

Steffens later preached in a sermon, "Mud or beauty—which do we look for as we journey through life? If we look for mud and ugliness, we find them—they are there. Just as the artist found beauty in the muddy river, because that is what he was looking for, we will find, in the stream of life, those things which we desire to see. To look for the best and see the beautiful is the way to get the best out of life each day."

Even the Bible says that what you see is what you get!

Finally, brethren, whatsoever things are true, whatsoever things are honest, whatsoever things are just, whatsoever things are pure, whatsoever things are lovely, whatsoever things are of good report; if there be any virtue, and if there be any praise, think on these things.

PHILIPPIANS 4:8

*The bridge you burn now
may be the one you
later have to cross.*

𝐼n *Learning to Forgive,* Doris Donnelly writes, "Some years ago I met a family very proficient in the use of scissors. . . . The friends of each family member were under constant scrutiny to determine whether they measured up to the standards imposed by mother and father. One slip . . . resulted in ostracism from the narrow circle of 'friends.' . . . Anyone who did not respond immediately with profuse gratitude was eliminated from the list for the next time. Snip.

"Eventually I, too, was scissored out of their lives. I never knew for sure why, but I knew enough to recognize that once I was snipped away there was no hope of my being sewn into their lives again.

"Last year the mother of the family died. The father and daughters, expecting large crowds to gather to say their final farewells, enlisted the assistance of the local police to handle traffic. . . . Telegrams were sent . . . phone calls were made . . . local motels were alerted . . . yet in the end, only the husband, the daughters, their husbands, and a grandchild or two attended the services."[12]

Cutting imperfect people out of our lives is a prescription for loneliness. Who would remain to be our friends? Is there anyone you could sew back into your pattern? Why not give them a call?

If it be possible, as much as lieth in you, live peaceably with all men.

ROMANS 12:18

*Real friends are those who,
when you've made a fool of
yourself, don't feel you've
done a permanent job.*

$\mathcal{N}$apoleon went to school in Brienne with
a young man named Demasis who greatly
admired him. After Napoleon quelled the mob in
Paris and served at Toulon, his authority was
stripped from him, and he became penniless. We
rarely think of Napoleon as struggling through
hard times. However, with thoughts of suicide, he
proceeded toward a bridge to throw himself into
the waters below. On the way he met his old
friend Demasis, who asked him what was troubling him.

Napoleon told him bluntly he was without
money, his mother was in need, and he despaired
of his situation ever changing. "Oh, if that is all,"

Demasis said, "take this; it will supply your wants." He put a pouch of gold into his hands and walked away. Normally Napoleon would have never taken such a handout, but that night he did, and his hope was renewed.

When Napoleon came to power, he sought far and wide to thank and promote his friend, but he never found him. It was rumored that Demasis lived and served in one of Napoleon's own armies, but never revealed his true identity; rather, he was content to serve quietly in support of the leader he admired.

Sometimes our simple words or deeds make all the difference in the world to someone who doesn't know where to turn.

Love . . . bears all things,
believes all things, hopes all things,
endures all things. Love never fails.

1 CORINTHIANS 13:7,8 NKJV

*Most people wish
to serve God—but only
in an advisory capacity.*

*F*or weeks, eight-year-old Susie had been looking forward to a particular Saturday fishing trip with her dad. But when the day finally arrived, it was raining heavily.

Susie wandered around the house all morning, grumbling as she peered out the windows, "Seems like the Lord would know it would have been better to have the rain yesterday than today." Her father tried to explain how important the rain was to the farmers and gardeners. But Susie only replied, "It just isn't fair."

Around three o'clock, the rain stopped. There was still time for fishing, so father and daughter quickly loaded their gear and headed for the lake. Because of the rainstorm, the fish were really biting. Within a couple of hours, they returned with a full stringer of fish.

At the family's fish dinner that night, Susie was asked to say grace. She concluded her prayer by saying, "And, Lord, if I sounded grumpy earlier today, it was because I couldn't see far enough ahead."

When we seek God's advice in our lives, it is important to realize He alone can see what's coming!

Humble yourselves therefore under the mighty hand of God, that he may exalt you in due time.

1 PETER 5:6

Conscience is God's built-in warning system. Be very happy when it hurts you. Be very worried when it doesn't.

*K*elley was surprised to find a hair dryer tucked into a corner of an old suitcase. For years she had used the case to store bits of fabric from her sewing projects. Now, while piecing together a quilt, she had unearthed it. *Where did this come from?* she asked herself.

After several days of trying to remember, she recalled having used it while visiting friends nearly a decade before. She had made several visits to the family and apparently had placed the borrowed hair dryer into her case inadvertently. To complicate matters, the family had asked about its whereabouts, and she had replied she didn't have a clue!

Embarrassed, she thought, *How can I tell my friends after all these years that I have this?* However, her conscience wouldn't let the matter rest. She finally sent the hair dryer back to the family with an apology and an explanation. With many laughs, all was quickly forgiven.

A healthy conscience is one of our greatest gifts from God. It serves to keep our lives on track and thus maintains peace in our hearts.

Herin do I exercise myself, to have always a conscience void of offense toward God, and toward men.

ACTS 24:16

If you don't stand for something you'll fall for anything!

$\mathcal{A}$ saleswoman passed a particular corner each day on her way to work. For more than a week she observed a young girl trying to sell a floppy-eared puppy. The saleswoman finally said to the girl, "Honey, if you really want to sell this dog, then I suggest you clean him up, brush his coat, raise your price, and make people think they're getting something big." At noon, the saleswoman noticed the girl had taken her advice. The puppy was groomed and sitting under a big sign: "TREEMENNDOUS Puppy for Sale—$5,000."

The saleswoman smiled and gulped, determined to tell the girl later that she may have overpriced the puppy. To her surprise, on the way home she saw the puppy was gone!

Flabbergasted, the woman sought out the girl to ask if she had really sold the dog for $5,000.

The girl replied, "I sure did, and I want to thank you for all your help." The saleswoman stuttered, "How in the world did you do it?" the girl said, "It was easy. I just took two $2,500 cats in exchange!"

Two thousand years ago there was another great exchange. On a cross outside Jerusalem, Jesus Christ gave His life in exchange for ours. What value did He see in us? We were His prized creation, stolen for a season by our own will, but now repurchased as His beloved possession.

Ye are bought with a price: therefore glorify God in your body, and in your spirit, which are God's.

1 CORINTHIANS 6:20

You should never let
adversity get you down—
except on your knees.

*M*any people see abundant spring rains as a great blessing to farmers, especially if the rains come after the plants have sprouted and are several inches tall. What they don't realize is even a short drought can have a devastating effect on a crop of seedlings that have received too much rain.

Why? Because during frequent rains, the young plants are not required to push their roots deeper into the soil in search of water. If a drought occurs later, plants with shallow root systems will quickly die.

We often receive abundance into our lives— rich fellowship, great teaching, thorough "soak-ings" of spiritual blessings. Yet, when stress or tragedy enters our lives, we may find ourselves thinking God has abandoned us or is unfaithful. The fact is, we have allowed the easiness of our lives to keep us from pushing our spiritual roots deeper. We have allowed others to spoon feed us, rather than developing our own deep, personal relationship with God through prayer and study of His Word.

Only the deeply rooted are able to endure hard times without wilting. The best advice is to enjoy the "rain" while seeking to grow even closer to Him.

I am persuaded, that neither death, nor life, nor angels, nor principalities, nor powers, nor things present, nor things to come . . . shall be able to separate us from the love of God, which is in Christ Jesus our Lord.

ROMANS 8:38,39

The best bridge between
hope and despair is often
a good night's sleep.

*M*edical researchers are coming to what
may seem to be a common sense conclusion: a
missing ingredient to health may be "vitamin
Zzzzzzzz."

When participants in one study were cheated
out of four hours of sleep for four consecutive
nights, they had on average a 30 percent drop in
their immune systems, as measured by natural
killer-cell activity. Such a drop can readily
increase a person's susceptibility to colds and flu,
and perhaps to other serious diseases. Says sleep
researcher Michael Irwin, M.D., "Many people
just need a regular-length sleep to get those
natural killer cells revved up again."

While a steady diet of sufficient sleep may
not completely prevent disease, it can improve

the body's defense system and help a person combat disease more efficiently and effectively.

Sleep is the cheapest health aid a person can take. Sleep is God's own means of restoring health to the body, as well as providing rest to the mind. Many have reported a new outlook or a change of heart after a good night's sleep.

Ask God to renew your strength as you sleep tonight, then get to bed on time so He can give you what you requested.

It is vain for you to rise up early, to sit up late, to eat the bread of sorrows: for so he giveth his beloved sleep.

PSALM 127:2

*It is good to remember
that the tea kettle, although
up to its neck in hot water,
continues to sing.*

$\mathcal{B}$ernard Gilpin was accused of heresy before Bishop Bonner, and shortly thereafter was sent to London for trial. Gilpin's favorite saying was, "All things are for the best." He set out on his journey with that attitude, but on his way fell from his horse and broke his leg.

"Is all for the best now?" a scorner said, mocking Gilpin for his optimism. "I still believe so, " he replied.

He turned out to be right. During the time he was convalescing from the accident, and before he was able to resume his journey, Queen Mary died. Consequently, the case against him was dropped. Instead of being burned at the stake, Gilpin returned home in triumph.

We tend to see all accidents and illness that come our way as misfortune caused by the enemy of our souls. That may not always be the case. Rather than spend our energy railing against bad times, perhaps we should direct our effort toward praising the One who promises to work all things together for the good of those who are called according to His purposes. (See Romans 8:28.) God has many methods and means for accomplishing His plan!

Rejoice evermore. In every thing give thanks: for this is the will of God in Christ Jesus concerning you.

1 THESSALONIANS 5:16,18

It's good to be a Christian and know it, but it's better to be a Christian and show it!

Before the colonialists imposed national boundaries, the kings of Laos and Vietnam had already reached an agreement about who was Laotian and who was Vietnamese. Those who ate short-grain rice, built their houses on stilts, and decorated their homes with Indian-style serpents were considered Laotians. Those who ate long-grain rice, built their houses on the ground, and decorated their homes with Chinese-style dragons were Vietnamese. The kings taxed the people accordingly, and had little use for boundaries apart from this designation.

The kings knew it was not the exact location of a person's home that determined their culture of loyalty. Instead, each person belonged to the kingdom whose values they shared.

So it is with a Christian. Regardless of our culture or nationality, we belong to God's kingdom. We live according to the values, standards, and commandments He has established. When we pray, "Thy kingdom come, Thy will be done," we are asking that the heavenly law of love become established in our lives here on earth. We are His people, regardless of our address.

*By this shall all men know
that ye are my disciples, if ye
have love one to another.*

JOHN 13:35

• 149 •

Sorrow looks back.
Worry looks around.
Faith looks up.

Can the Lord speak through a pop song? Fontella Bass thinks so. She was at the lowest ebb in her life during 1990. It had been twenty-five years since her rhythm and blues single had hit number one on the charts. She had no career to speak of, and she was broke, tired, and cold. The only heat in her house came from a gas stove in the kitchen. She had also strayed far from the church where she started singing gospel songs as a child.

Fontella says, "I said a long prayer. I said, 'I need to see a sign to continue on.'" No sooner had she prayed than she heard her hit song, "Rescue Me," on a television commercial. To her, it was as if "the Lord had stepped right into my world!"

Fontella was unaware American Express had been using her song as part of a commercial, and officials had been unable to locate her to pay royalties. Not only did she receive back-royalties, but new opportunities began to open for her to sing.

She released a new album entitled "No Ways Tired," but the best news is that she renewed her relationship with God. "For so many years I tried doing it on my own, and it didn't work," she says. "Then I took it out of my hands and turned it over to Him, and now everything's happening."[13]

Fixing our eyes on Jesus, the author and perfecter of faith, who for the joy set before Him endured the cross, despising the shame, and has sat down at the right hand of the throne of God.

HEBREWS 12:2 NASB

Sometimes we are so busy adding up our troubles that we forget to count our blessings.

*I*n some parts of Mexico, hot springs and cold springs are found side by side. Because of this natural phenomenon, local women have the convenience of boiling their clothes in the hot springs, then rinsing them in the adjacent cold springs. While watching this procedure a number of years ago, a tourist said to her guide, "I imagine that they think old Mother Nature is pretty generous to supply such ample, clean hot and cold water here side by side for their free use."

The guide replied, "Well, actually, no. There is much grumbling because Mother Nature supplies no soap! And not only that, but the rumor has started to filter in that there are machines that do this work in other parts of the world."

So often we compare our lives to others—what they have in contrast to what we don't have and what they are that we aren't. Such comparisons invariably leave us feeling left out, rejected, and cheated. If we aren't careful to put the brakes on such negative emotions, we can become unnecessarily bitter.

Count your blessings today! If you own one, start with a washing machine.

I will remember the works of the LORD: surely I will remember thy wonders of old. I will meditate also of all thy work, and talk of thy doings.

PSALM 77:11,12

God can heal a broken heart, but
He has to have all the pieces.

*S*o many things of beauty begin as "bits and pieces"—not unlike our lives, which often seem like jigsaw puzzles with a multitude of scattered pieces.

Or the artist's collage.

Or a stained glass window.

Or a mosaic floor.

Tragedies and pain can strike any person, and we need to allow the Master Craftsman to put us back together according to His design, rather than trying to find all the pieces and glue ourselves together without Him.

In *The Dark Night of the Soul,* Georgia Harkness writes, "The Christian faith imparts meaning to life. A living faith that is centered in God as revealed in Christ takes our chaotic, disorganized selves, with their crude jumble of pleasures and pains, and knits them together into a steadiness and joy that can endure anything with God."[14]

Trust God today to turn your brokenness into something of beauty and value.

My son, give me thine heart.

PROVERBS 23:26

*Be more concerned with what
God thinks about you than
what people think about you.*

$\mathcal{A}$ pastor's wife was amazed when she heard a person say, "One hour is only 4 percent of a day." She had not thought about time in this way. Sensing the need for more prayer time in her life, she thought surely she could give God at least 4 percent of her time. She determined to try it.

Rather than try to fit prayer into her schedule, she decided to fix a prayer time, and then fit the rest of the day around it. At the time, her children were old enough to travel to school alone. By 8:30 each morning, a hush fell over her home. She knew her best hour for prayer would be between 8:30 and 9:30 A.M. To guarantee she was uninterrupted, she made it known in the parish that, except for emergencies, she would be grateful if people didn't call her until 9:30 in the morning.

To her surprise, no one in the church was offended. Instead they responded very positively. Several other women began to follow her example by setting aside the same hour to pray every day!

When we seek God's plan first, all our plans with other people will have a way of falling into place.

Seek first the kingdom of God and His righteousness, and all these things shall be added to you.

MATTHEW 6:33 NKJV

The best way to get the last word is to apologize.

*I*n 1755 a twenty-three-year-old colonel was in the midst of running for a seat in the Virginia assembly when he made an insulting remark as part of a campaign speech. The remark was addressed to a hot-tempered man named Payne, who responded by knocking the colonel down with a hickory stick. Soldiers rushed to the colonel's assistance, and it appeared that a full-blown fight would ensue. But the would-be politician got up, dusted himself off, called off the soldiers, and left the scene.

The next morning the colonel wrote Payne, requesting his presence at a local tavern. Payne obliged, but wondered what motives and demands the colonel might make—perhaps an apology or even a duel. To Payne's surprise, the colonel met him with an apology, asking forgiveness for his derogatory remarks and offering a handshake.

The move may have been viewed by others as politically expedient, but Colonel George Washington considered it personally imperative if he was to enjoy internal peace as he continued with his campaign.

The moment we feel like demanding forgiveness from others may be the moment when we are to forgive.

If you have been trapped by what you said, ensnared by the words of your mouth, then do this, my son, to free yourself, since you have fallen into your neighbor's hands: Go and humble yourself; press your plea with your neighbor!

PROVERBS 6:2,3 NIV

Forget yourself for others and others will not forget you!

*M*illie was a mentally retarded adult who lived with her mother in a small town. She was known for her proverbial "green thumb" as a gardener. Lawns, hedges, and flower beds flourished under her loving attention. Millie also volunteered by cutting grass and weeds, raking leaves, and planting flowers in vacant lots throughout the town. She was known for her oil can. She always carried a small can of lubricating oil in her hip pocket and applied a dose of oil to any squeaky door, hinge, or gate she encountered.

On Sundays Millie went to church with her mother. When teased, she refused to respond in any way other than with good humor and unflappable cheer.

When Millie died, everyone in town showed up for her funeral. There were scores who traveled from distant places to attend, including many of those who had once teased her.

Without consciously attempting to do so, Millie exemplified good citizenship. She worked hard, was an optimist, eased tensions, and was a faithful church member.

Others really do notice the small things we do for them in love and kindness.

Therefore all things whatsoever
ye would that men should do
to you, do ye even so to them: for
this is the law and the prophets.

MATTHEW 7:12

• 161 •

The secret of contentment
is the realization that
life is a gift, not a right.

*F*ormer nationally syndicated columnist and current author, Anna Quindlen, seems to have enjoyed success at everything she has attempted. But in taking a fellow commentator to task after he made light of teenage problems, Anna was reminded of the two attempts to end her own life she had made at age sixteen. She writes, "I was really driven through my high school years. I always had to be perfect in every way, ranging from how I looked to how my grades were. It was too much pressure."

In the early 1970s, Anna's mother died from ovarian cancer. This tragedy cured Anna from any desire to commit suicide. Her attitude toward life changed. "I could never look at life as anything but a great gift. I realized I didn't have any business taking it for granted."[15]

It is only when we recognize life as "temporary" that we truly come to grips with what is important. When we face our own immortality, our priorities quickly come into focus.

Consider your life as God's gift to you. Every moment is precious, so cherish each one. In doing so, you'll find purpose and meaning for each day.

*Godliness with contentment
is great gain. For we brought
nothing into this world, and it is
certain we can carry nothing out.*

1 TIMOTHY 6:6,7

Those who bring sunshine to the lives of others cannot keep it from themselves.

There was a wealthy noblewoman who had grown tired of life. She had everything one could wish for except happiness and contentment. She said, "I am weary of life. I will go to the river and there end my life."

As she walked along, she felt a little hand tugging at her skirts. Looking down, she saw a frail, hungry-looking little boy who pleaded, "There are six of us. We are dying for want of food!" The noblewoman thought, *Why should I not relieve this wretched family? I have the means, and it seems I will have no more use for riches when I am gone.*

Following the little boy, she entered a scene of misery, sickness, and want. She opened her purse and emptied its contents. The family members were beside themselves with joy and gratitude. Even more taken with their need, the noblewoman said, "I'll return tomorrow, and I will share with you more of the good things which God has given to me in abundance!"

She left that scene of want and wretchedness rejoicing that the child had found her. For the first time in her life she understood the reason for her wealth. Never again did she think of ending her life, which was now filled with meaning and purpose.

Be not deceived; God is not mocked: for whatsoever a man soweth, that shall he also reap.

GALATIANS 6:7

It's the little things in life that determine the big things.

*I*n speaking to a group of ministers, Fred Craddock noted the importance of being faithful in the little things of life. He said: "To give my life for Christ appears glorious. To pour myself out for others . . . to pay the ultimate price of martyrdom—I'll do it. I'm ready, Lord, to go out in a blaze of glory."

"We think giving our all to the Lord is like taking a $1,000 bill and laying it on the table— 'Here's my life, Lord. I'm giving it all.'

"But the reality for most of us is that He sends us to the bank and has us cash in the $1,000 for quarters. We go through life putting out twenty-five cents here and fifty cents there. Listen to the neighbor kid's troubles instead of saying, 'Get lost.' Go to a committee meeting.

Give a cup of water to a shaky old man in a nursing home.

"Usually giving our life to Christ isn't glorious. It's done in all those little acts of love, twenty-five cents at a time. It would be easy to go out in a flash of glory; it's harder to live the Christian life little by little over the long haul."[16]

Ask the Lord to show you how you can spend your life well.

Thou hast been faithful over a few things, I will make thee ruler over many things: enter thou into the joy of thy lord.

MATTHEW 25:21

Contentment isn't getting what we want but being satisfied with what we have.

*I*n a matter of seconds, Vickie's life was shattered. A trapeze artist, she lost control of the flybar one day and careened headfirst into the net. She broke her neck between the fifth and sixth cervical vertebrae and became paralyzed, a quadriplegic.

Three years after the accident, she had fallen into deep despair and self-pity and was determined to take her life. Her attempt failed, and she ended up in a psychiatric hospital. On the fourth anniversary of her fall, she and her husband separated. Bitterness set in.

One day a Christian home health aide was assigned to her. Mae Lynne introduced Vickie to Jesus Christ and the Bible. Vickie began to learn to "stand firm" in her faith and to "walk" in obedience to God.

A minister faithfully taught her for two years. Then Vickie began a ministry of encouragement by writing a dozen letters each week to prison inmates and others with disabilities. She now says, "Quadriplegics aren't supposed to have this much joy, are they?"[17]

Vickie still uses a wheelchair, becomes dizzy at times, has occasional respiratory problems, and needs an attendant's care. However, she has deep inner strength because of her relationship with Jesus. Now others describe her as "a fountain of smiles."

Not that I speak in respect of want: for I have learned, in whatsoever state I am, therewith to be content.

PHILIPPIANS 4:11

God plus one is always a majority!

Cardinal von Faulhaber of Munich is reported once to have had a conversation with the famed physicist Albert Einstein.

"Cardinal von Faulhaber," Einstein said, "I respect religion, but I believe in mathematics. Probably it is the other way around with you."

"You are mistaken," replied the Cardinal. "To me, both are merely different expressions of the same divine exactness."

"But, your Eminence, what would you say if mathematical science should someday come to conclusions directly contradictory to religious beliefs?"

"Oh," the Cardinal answered with ease, "I have the highest respect for the competence of mathematicians. I am sure they would never rest until they discovered their mistake."

Regardless of how ardently some people try to suppress it, God's truth will always prevail.

If God be for us,
who can be against us?

ROMANS 8:31

*Whoever gossips to you
will be a gossip of you.*

*L*aura Ingalls Wilder writes in *Little House in the Ozarks:* "I know a little band of friends that calls itself a woman's club. The avowed purpose of this club is study, but there is an undercurrent of deeper, truer things than even culture and self-improvement. There is no obligation, and there are no promises; but in forming the club and in selecting new members, only those are chosen who are kind-hearted and dependable as well as the possessors of a certain degree of intelligence and a small amount of the genius which is the capacity for careful work. In short, those who are taken into membership are those who will make good friends, and so they are a little band who are each for all and all for each. . . .

"They are getting so in the habit of speaking good words that I expect to see them all develop into Golden Gossips.

"Ever hear of golden gossip? I read of it some years ago. A woman who was always talking about her friends and neighbors made it her business to talk of them, in fact, never said anything but good of them. She was a gossip, but it was 'golden gossip.' This woman's club seems to be working in the same way."[18]

Who wouldn't enjoy belonging to such a club?

A talebearer revealeth secrets:
but he that is of a faithful
spirit concealeth the matter.

PROVERBS 11:13

Jesus is a friend who knows all your faults and still loves you anyway.

*A*t a crucial transition time a Christian woman cried out to the Lord, despairing over the lack of spiritual power and fruitfulness she was experiencing in her life. Suddenly she sensed Jesus standing beside her, asking, "May I have the keys to your life?"

The experience was so realistic, the woman reached into her pocket and took out a ring of keys. "Are all the keys here?" the Lord asked.

"Yes, except the key to one small room in my life."

"If you cannot trust Me in all rooms of your life, I cannot accept any of the keys."

The woman was so overwhelmed at the thought of the Lord moving out of her life altogether, she cried, "Lord, take the keys to all the rooms of my life!"

Many of us have rooms we hope no one will ever see. We intend to clean them out someday, but "someday" never seems to come. When we invite Jesus into these rooms, He will help us clean them. With Him, we have the courage to throw away all the "junk," and fill the rooms with His love and peace and joy.

God commendeth his love toward us, in that, while we were yet sinners, Christ died for us.

ROMANS 5:8

*Every person should have
a special cemetery lot in
which to bury the faults of
friends and loved ones.*

A much-loved minister of God once
carried a secret burden of long-past sin buried
deep in his heart. He had committed the sin
many years before during his seminary training.
No one knew what he had done, but they did
know he had repented. Even so, he had suffered
years of remorse over the incident without any
sense of God's forgiveness.

A woman in his church deeply loved God and
claimed to have visions in which Jesus Christ
spoke to her. The minister, skeptical of her
claims, asked of her, "The next time you speak to
the Lord, would you please ask Him what sin

your minister committed while he was in seminary." The woman agreed.

When she came to the church a few days later the minister asked, "Did He visit you?" She said, "Yes."

"And did you ask Him what sin I committed in seminary?"

"Yes, I asked Him," she replied.

"Well, what did He say?"

"He said, 'I don't remember.'"

Be ye kind one to another,
tenderhearted, forgiving one
another, even as God for
Christ's sake hath forgiven you.

EPHESIANS 4:32

A minute of thought is worth more than an hour of talk.

A heart doctor was amazed at the great improvement one of his patients had made. When he had seen the woman a few months earlier, she was seriously ill in the hospital, needing an oxygen mask. He asked the woman what had happened.

The woman said, "I was sure the end was near and that you and your staff had given up hope. However, Thursday morning when you entered with your troops, something happened that changed everything. You listened to my heart; you seemed pleased by the finding, and you announced to all those standing about my bed that I had a 'wholesome gallop.' I knew that the doctors, in talking to me, might try to soften things. But I knew they wouldn't kid each other. So when I overheard you tell your colleagues I had a wholesome gallop, I figured I still had a lot of kick to my heart and could not be dying. My spirits were for the first time lifted, and I knew I would live and recover."

The heart doctor never told the woman that a third-sound gallop is a poor sign that denotes the heart muscle is straining and usually failing!

Just a few words can be enough to make a difference in a person's life. How important it is to choose our words wisely!

Set a watch, O LORD, before my mouth; keep the door of my lips.

PSALM 141:3

*You can win more friends with
your ears than with your mouth.*

*D*ale Carnegie, author of *How To Win
Friends and Influence People,* is considered one of
the greatest "friend winners" of the century. He
taught, "You can make more friends in two
months by becoming interested in other people
than you can in two years by trying to get other
people interested in you."

To illustrate his point, Carnegie would tell
how dogs have learned the fine art of making
friends better than most people. When you get
within ten feet of a friendly dog, he will begin to
wag his tail, a visible sign that he welcomes and
enjoys your presence. If you take time to pet the
dog, he will become excited, lick you, and jump
all over you to show how much he appreciates
you. The dog became man's best friend by being
genuinely interested in people!

One of the foremost ways, of course, in which we show our interest in others is to listen to them—to ask questions, to intently listen to their answers, and to ask further questions based upon what they say. The person who feels "heard" is likely to seek out his friendly listener again and again, and to count that person as a great friend.

Need a friend? Start listening with your heart.

Let every man be swift to hear, slow to speak, slow to wrath.

JAMES 1:19

It's not the outlook but
the uplook that counts.

The story of Helen Keller is well known. Deaf and blind from a childhood disease, her teacher, Anne Sullivan, opened the world to her through the other senses of taste, touch, and smell. In her autobiography, Helen Keller wrote:

"Fate—silent, pitiless—bars the way. Fain would I question his imperious decree; for my heart is undisciplined and passionate, but my tongue will not utter the bitter, futile words that rise to my lips, and they fall back into my heart like unshed tears. Silence sits immense upon my soul. Then comes hope with a smile and whispers, 'There is joy in self-forgetfulness.' So I try to make the light in other people's eyes my sun, the music in others' ears my symphony, the smile on others' lips my happiness."

How sad it is when we search only within ourselves for a reason to be happy, because the happiness in those around us is reason enough to have joy, regardless of our situation or handicap. And, if the poor and the handicapped can have joy, how can we wallow in depression?

If we look to Jesus, all will be well with us—inside and out.

Looking unto Jesus the author
and finisher of our faith.

HEBREWS 12:2

It isn't hard to make a
mountain out of a molehill.
Just add a little dirt.

*S*usan was deeply disappointed at the lack
of emotional closeness she felt in her marriage.
She began to lash out at her husband. He, of
course, reacted with his own defensive anger.
Over time their anger grew, threats were
exchanged, and eventually divorce became part of
their confrontations. Finally, Susan's husband
moved out and she filed for divorce.

The divorce proceedings were bitter. They
fought all the way through it. When they met to
sign the final papers, they stopped to look at
each other, and Susan saw in his eyes the very
feelings she was experiencing—a feeling of
longing and yet of resignation. She thought, *I
don't want to divorce him, and I don't think he
wants to divorce me.*

She voiced her thoughts to her husband, and for a moment it appeared he might also soften and admit he, too, still cared. But then he said in a dull monotone, "We've come this far, I guess we should finish it." Susan left the courtroom realizing she had never really wanted a divorce. She just wanted her husband to listen.

Don't allow anger to lead you anywhere, but especially down a road you truly don't want to travel.

Starting a quarrel is like breaching a dam; so drop the matter before a dispute breaks out.

PROVERBS 17:14 NIV

The art of being a good guest is knowing when to leave.

*I*t has been said that fish and house guests have one thing in common—after three days they both begin to stink. Depending on the circumstances, a stay may not require that much time before it "goes bad." Generally speaking, the more displaced your hostess has made herself on your account, the shorter your stay should be. Be certain before you visit with relatives or friends that you both know when you will arrive and when you will depart. The old entertainer's rule of thumb, "Leave them wanting more" is good advice for a house guest.

The same goes for shorter visits—better to leave earlier than later. When the hostess begins to yawn or gather up the dishes, take the hint!

George Washington visited the home of friends one evening, and when the hour came for him to leave, he said good-bye to the adults, then paused at the entrance where a little girl opened the door to let him out. Washington bowed to her and said, "I am sorry, my little dear, to give you so much trouble."

She replied, "I wish, sir, it was to let you in." Now that's a welcome guest!

Withdraw thy foot from thy neighbour's house; lest he be weary of thee, and so hate thee.

PROVERBS 25:17

*Jesus is a friend who walks in
when the world has walked out.*

While serving in India, a devout English judge befriended a young Indian man. Having been raised in a prominent Indian family, he had been cast out after he converted to Christianity. The judge took the boy into his household where he happily worked as a house boy.

It was the custom of the household to have a devotional time every evening. One night the judge read aloud the words of Jesus: "Every one that hath forsaken houses, or brethren, or sisters, or father, or mother, or wife, or children, or lands, for my name's sake, shall receive a hundredfold." (Matthew 19:29).

The judge turned to the lad and said, "Noboby here has done this except you, Norbudur. Will you tell us, is it true what Jesus has said?"

The young Indian man read the verse aloud for himself and then turned to the family and said, "No, there is an error."

Startled the judge responded, "There is?"

The youth replied, "It says He gives a hundredfold. I know He gives a thousandfold."

With eternal life, intimacy with the Father, and all the riches of Heaven, who can truly measure the value of what it means when Jesus Christ comes into a person's life?

These things I have spoken unto you, that in me ye might have peace. In the world ye shall have tribulation: but be of good cheer; I have overcome the world.

JOHN 16:33

Those who deserve love the least need it the most.

On their way back from a meeting of the Greek Orthodox Archdiocese, Father Demetrios Frangos and Father Germanos Stavropoulos were in a car accident. A young woman high on PCP drove into their car while they waited at a stoplight, and both priests were killed instantly. The woman, a legal secretary with a seven-year-old, had no previous police record, but admitted to having used drugs for ten years. She was charged with murder and several other felonies. The tabloid headlines were especially vicious, referring to her as the "priest killer."

Father Demetrios' son, George, responded with forgiveness, not anger. He offered to help provide the woman with a lawyer and hoped if she was convicted the sentence would be short. He said, "The last thing my father would have wanted was to make an example [of her]. This woman is anguished and troubled to begin with . . . we have to look after the innocent one, the child. It is extremely important that her child be told that we forgive her mother."[19]

George Frangos loved his father and grieved for him, but more important to him than "legal justice" was "divine justice"—that this woman and her little daughter know the love of Jesus Christ.

I say unto you, Love your enemies; bless them that curse you, do good to them that hate you, and pray for them which despitefully use you.

MATTHEW 5:44

*Faith is daring the soul to go
beyond what the eyes can see.*

Sometimes I'm sad. I know not why
My heart is sore and distressed;
It seems the burdens of this world
Have settled on my heart.
And yet I know . . . I know that God
Who doeth all things right
Will lead me thus to understand
To walk by FAITH . . . not SIGHT.
And though I may not see the way
He's planned for me to go . . .
That way seems dark to me just now
But oh, I'm sure He knows!
Today He guides my feeble step
Tomorrow's in His right . . .
He has asked me to never fear . . .
But walk by FAITH . . . not SIGHT.
Some day the mists will roll away,

The sun will shine again.
I'll see the beauty in the flowers
I'll hear the bird's refrain.
And then I'll know my Father's hand
Has led the way to light
Because I placed my hands in His
And walked by FAITH . . . not SIGHT.

—Ruth A. Morgan[20]

We walk by faith, not by sight.

2 CORINTHIANS 5:7

A critical spirit is like poison ivy—it only takes a little contact to spread the poison.

$\mathcal{A}$ little girl once asked her father how wars got started.

"Well," said her father, "suppose America persisted in quarreling with England, and. . . . "

"But," interrupted her mother, "America must never quarrel with England."

"I know," said the father, "but I am only using a hypothetical instance."

"But you are misleading the child," protested Mom.

"No, I am not," replied the father indignantly, with an edge of anger in his tone.

"Never mind, Daddy," the little girl interjected, "I think I know how wars get started."

Most major arguments don't begin large, but are rooted in a small annoyance, breach, or trespass. It's like the mighty oak that stood on the skyline of the Rocky Mountains. The tree had survived hail, heavy snows, bitter cold, and ferocious storms for more than a century. It was finally felled not by a great lightning strike or an avalanche, but by an attack of tiny beetles.

A little hurt, neglect, or insult can be the beginning of the end for virtually any relationship. Therefore, take care what you say and be certain the attitude you have is right!

Avoid worldly and empty chatter,
for it will lead to further ungodliness.

2 TIMOTHY 2:16 NASB

Two things are hard on the heart—running upstairs and running down people.

Wouldn't his world be better,
If folks whom we meet would say,
"I know something good about you,"
And treat you just that way?
Wouldn't it be splendid,
If each handshake, good and true,
Carried with it this assurance:
"I know something good about you?"
Wouldn't life be happier,
If the good that's in us all,
Were the only thing about us
That people would recall?
Wouldn't our days be sweeter,
If we praised the good we see?
For there is a lot of goodness,
In the worst of you and me.

Wouldn't it be fine to practice,
This way of thinking too;
You know something good about me,
I know something good about you?[21]

Since we can never know or tell the full story about any other human being, why not just skip to the good highlights?

Let no corrupt communication
proceed out of your mouth,
but that which is good to the
use of edifying, that it may
minister grace unto the hearers.

EPHESIANS 4:29

● 197 ●

Humor is to life what shock absorbers are to automobiles.

On a hot June day, Winona and Will had just exchanged their wedding vows and were about to take their triumphant wedding march back down the aisle. Suddenly Winona's six-foot-tall brother—a groomsman—fainted, and not very delicately at that. In the course of his falling, he toppled another groomsman and lurched against the best man, nearly forcing him down too. Two attendants each grabbed an arm of the fallen man and dragged him out of the church, in full view of the three hundred guests and a horrified young bride.

Winona had no doubt her wedding was ruined and she would be the laughingstock of the town. It was all she could do to keep back the tears as she walked down the aisle with Will. As they neared the back of the church, however, Will burst into laughter—a big, booming, infectious laugh—and Winona had to laugh too. Soon the entire church was guffawing with gusto.

Winona said many years later, " My first reaction to nearly any situation used to be 'Oh, no,' but Will's first reaction has always been to see humor in a situation. I've grown to adopt his point of view. I figure the very least I can glean from a nightmare is a good laugh and a memorable story to tell later."[22]

Then our mouth was filled with laughter, and our tongue with singing. Then they said among the nations, "The Lord has done great things for them."

PSALM 126:2 NKJV

*Kindness is the oil that takes
the friction out of life.*

A number of years ago, the Advertising and Sales Executive Club sponsored a Courtesy Campaign in Kansas City. One thousand silver dollars were flown in from Denver. Then, over a period of days, "mystery shoppers: visited all types of stores, banks, and other places of business. They listened to telephone operators and observed bus and street-car drivers. Each day they filed a written report on the persons they found to be the most courteous.

Those chosen as the most courteous people in the city received a silver dollar, along with a "courtesy pays" button and a congratulatory card. The fifteen most outstandingly courteous people were guests at the banquet, where they were awarded $25 each. In all, more than 100 people were honored.

What resulted was not only a temporary increase in the courtesy of the local residents, but an awareness throughout the city that simple kindness is a nice thing with which to live! The "residual effect" remained long after the campaign, to the point where Kansas City is still regarded as one of the friendliest cities in the nation.

It doesn't cost anything to be kind, but kindness can pay off in big ways quite apart from money.

The fruit of the Spirit is . . . kindness.

GALATIANS 5:22 NIV

Our days are identical suitcases—all the same size— but some people can pack more into them than others.

Mary Smith went to church one Sunday morning and winced when she heard the organist miss a note during the processional. She noted a teenager talking while everybody was supposed to be in prayer. She also couldn't help but notice that several blooms in the altar bouquets were wilted. She felt the usher was scrutinizing what every person was putting into the offering plate, which made her angry. She counted at least five grammatical errors made by the preacher in his sermon. As she left the church through the side door after the closing hymn, she thought, *What a careless group of people!*

Amy Jones went to church one Sunday morning and was thrilled at the arrangement she heard of "A Mighty Fortress." Her heart was touched at hearing a teenager read the morning Scripture lesson. She was encouraged to see the church take up an offering to help hungry children in Nigeria. The preacher's sermon answered a question that had bothered her for some time. She felt radiant joy from the choir members during the recessional. She left the church thinking, *What a wonderful place to worship God!*

Mary and Amy went to the same church, on the same Sunday morning.

Be very careful, then, how you live—not as unwise but as wise, making the most of every opportunity.

EPHESIANS 5:15,16 NIV

*To forgive is to set a
prisoner free and discover
the prisoner was you.*

Meredith was surprised to find a letter in
her mailbox from her brother, Tim. It had been
three years since she had spoken to him, even
though they lived in the same town. In the letter,
Tom told her he and his wife were expecting
twins and he hoped she would come to visit the
babies after they were born. He expressed his
sorrow that they had not communicated more,
and apologized for whatever it was he had done
to cause them to be estranged.

Meredith's initial reaction was one of anger.
"Whatever it was?" Didn't he know? She immediately sat down and wrote a five-page letter detail-
ing all the wrongs Tim had committed that hurt
her. The phone rang, however, before she could
put her letter in an envelope, and it was several

hours before she returned to her writing desk. Upon rereading her letter, she was horrified at what she found.

She had thought she was being very matter of fact, but her words were full of anger and pain. Tears of forgiveness filled her eyes. *Perhaps it wasn't all Tom's fault.*

She called him the next day to say, "I can hardly wait to be the aunt of twins!"

If ye forgive men their trespasses, your heavenly Father will also forgive you: But if ye forgive not men their trespasses, neither will your Father forgive your trespasses.

MATTHEW 6:14,15

The heart is the happiest when it beats for others.

*A*lbert Einstein once reflected on the purpose of man's existence: "Strange is our situation here upon earth. Each of us comes for a short visit, not knowing why, yet sometimes seeming to a divine purpose. From the standpoint of daily life, however, there is one thing we do know: That we are here for the sake of others . . . for the countless unknown souls with whose fate we are connected by a bond of sympathy. Many times a day, I realize how much my own outer and inner life is built upon the labors of people, both living and dead, and how earnestly I must exert myself in order to give in return as much as I have received."

When we truly take stock of our lives, we must admit we have done nothing solely on our own. Our thinking has been fashioned by our many teachers and mentors, including family members. Our ability to function physically is the result, in part, of our genetic code and the productivity of others in providing food, water, and shelter. Our spiritual lives are a gift of God Himself. We are what we have received.

Our reaction to these facts drives each of us to give to others the good things we have been fortunate to receive. This is what being a citizen of God's kingdom is all about.

Greater love hath no man than this, that a man lay down his life for his friends.

JOHN 15:13

*A true friend never gets
in your way unless you
happen to be going down.*

OnE evening when a woman was driving
home, she noticed a truck driving very close
behind her. She stepped on the gas to put a little
distance between them, but when she sped up,
the truck did too. The faster she drove, the faster
he drove.

Frightened at being pursued this way, she got
off the freeway, but the truck followed her. She
turned up a main street, hoping to lose him in
traffic, but he even ran a red light in pursuit.
Finally, near the point of panic, she pulled into a
service station and bolted out of her car screaming for help. She was horrified to see the truck
driver spring from his vehicle and run toward her.

But then . . . not even looking at her, he
yanked open the back door of her vehicle and

pulled out a man who was hiding on the floor of her back seat.

Her pursuer had not been the real potential for danger in her life! The truck driver had spotted the man, a convicted rapist, leaving a café and hiding in her car shortly before she returned. His chase was not an effort to harm her, but to save her, even at the risk of his own life.

We often find true, faithful friends in those who have been close to us for years, but rarely in strangers.

A friend loves at all times, and a brother is born for adversity.

PROVERBS 17:17 NASB

*Laughter is the brush
that sweeps away the
cobwebs of the heart.*

*I*n *Growing Strong in the Seasons of Life,*
Charles Swindoll writes: "Tonight was fun 'n'
games night around the supper table in our
house. It was wild. First of all, one of the kids
snickered during the prayer (which isn't that
unusual), and that tipped the first domino. Then
a humorous incident from school was shared, and
the event (as well as how it was told) triggered
havoc around the table. That was the beginning
of twenty to thirty minutes of the loudest, silliest,
most enjoyable laughter you can imagine. At one
point I watched my oldest literally fall off his
chair in hysterics, my youngest doubled over in
his chair as his face wound up in his plate with
corn chips stuck to his cheeks . . . and my two
girls leaning back, lost and preoccupied in the

most beautiful and beneficial therapy God ever granted humanity: *laughter.*

"What is so amazing is that everything seemed far less serious and heavy. Irritability and impatience were ignored like unwanted guests. For example, during the meal little Chuck spilled his drink twice . . . and even *that* brought the house down. If I remember correctly, that made six times during the day he accidentally spilled his drink, but nobody bothered to count."[23]

Laughter—what a treasure it is!

A happy heart is good medicine and a cheerful mind works healing, but a broken spirit dries up the bones.

PROVERBS 17:22 AMP

*God has a history of
using the insignificant to
accomplish the impossible.*

*I*n order to communicate among themselves, Serbian shepherd boys developed an
ingenious system. They would stick the blades of
their long knives into the ground of a pasture,
and when one of the boys sensed an approaching
cattle thief, he would strike the handle of his
knife sharply. The vibration created a signal that
could be picked up by other shepherd boys, their
ears pressed tightly against the ground. It was by
this unique system that they outwitted thieves
who tried to creep up on their flocks and herds
under the cover of darkness and tall corn.

Most of the shepherd boys grew up and
forgot about their ground signals, but one boy
remembered. Twenty-five years after he left the
pastures, he made one of the greatest inventions

of the modern era. Michael Pupin changed the telephone from a device used only to speak across a city to a long-distance instrument that could be heard across a continent.

Something you take for granted today, something others may consider to be insignificant or ordinary, may actually become your key to greatness. Look around you. What is it that God has put at your disposal?

Jesus looking upon them saith,
With men it is impossible,
but not with God: for with
God all things are possible.

MARK 10:27

• 213 •

People may doubt what you say, but they will always believe what you do.

You may bring to your office, and put in a frame,

a motto as fine as its paint,

but if you're a crook when you're playing the game,

that motto won't make you a saint. You can stick up the placards all over the wall,

but here is a word I announce:

It is not the motto that hangs on the wall,

but the motto you live, that counts.

If the motto says, "Smile," and you carry a frown:

"Do it now," and you linger and wait;

if the motto says "Help," and you trample men down;

if the motto says, "Love," and you hate—

you won't get away with the mottoes you stall,
for truth will come forth with a bounce.
It is not the motto that hangs on the wall,
but the motto you live, that counts.[24]

*The tree is known and recognized
and judged by its fruit.*

MATTHEW 12:33 AMP

*Kindness is a language
which the deaf can hear
and the blind can see.*

"*I* often have thought that we are a little old-fashioned here in the Ozark hills," writes Laura Ingalls Wilder in *Little House in the Ozarks*. "Now I know we are, because we had a 'working' in our neighborhood this winter. That is a blessed, old-fashioned way of helping out a neighbor.

"While the winter was warm, still it has been much too cold to be without firewood; and this neighbor, badly crippled with rheumatism, was not able to get up his winter's wood. . . . So the men of the neighborhood gathered together one morning and dropped in on him. With cross-cut saws and axes, they took possession of his wood lot. . . . By night there was enough wood ready . . . to last the rest of the winter.

"The women did their part, too. All morning they kept arriving with well-filled baskets, and at noon a long table was filled with a country neighborhood dinner. . . . When the dishes were washed, they sewed, knit, crocheted, and talked for the rest of the afternoon. It was a regular old-fashioned good time, and we all went home with the feeling expressed by a newcomer when he said, 'Don't you know I'm proud to live in a neighborhood like this where they turn out and help one another when it's needed.' "[25]

His merciful kindness is great toward us: and the truth of the LORD endureth for ever. Praise ye the LORD.

PSALM 117:2

I make it a rule of Christian duty never to go to a place where there is not room for my Master as well as myself.

An attractive single woman had a job that required her to travel a great deal. When a new female colleague was added to her department, she told her how happy she was to have another woman on the team. She related how she often felt isolated when she found herself the only woman at breakfast in a hotel restaurant, or one of only a handful of women on a commuter flight.

"Do the men ever bother you?" the new young colleague asked.

"Rarely," the woman replied.

"Wow," said the young colleague. "You are so beautiful, I would think you are approached a great deal by men you really don't care to meet."

"No," the woman explained, "I just say five words, and immediately I am left alone."

"Five words?" the young colleague asked, hoping to gain a valuable tip. "What are they?"

"When I am approached by a man," the woman said, "I simply ask, 'Are you a born-again Christian?'"

"Has anyone ever said 'yes'?" the younger asked.

"Rarely," said the woman. "And when such men want to talk to me anyway, I always have an enjoyable conversation, because Jesus can be part of it."

Don't be teamed with those who do not love the Lord . . . How can a Christian be a partner with one who doesn't believe?

2 CORINTHIANS 6:14,15 TLB

Jesus can turn water into wine, but He can't turn your whining into anything.

*R*ather than whining that we don't have certain things in our lives or that something is wrong, we need to take positive action. Here are four steps toward turning whining into thanksgiving.

1. *Give something away.* When you give something you create both a physical and a mental space for something new and better to come into your life. Although you may think you are "lacking" something in life, when you give you demonstrate you have abundance to spare.

2. *Narrow your goals.* Don't expect everything good to come into you life all at once. When you focus your expectations toward specific and reachable goals, you

are more apt to direct your time and energy toward reaching them.

3. *Change your vocabulary from "I need" to "I want."* Most of the things we think we need are actually things we want. When you receive them, you are more likely to be thankful for them as luxuries rather than necessities.

4. *Choose to be thankful for what you already have.* Thanksgiving is a choice we make. Every one of us has more things to be thankful for than we could begin to recount in a day.

Do all things without murmurings and disputings.

PHILIPPIANS 2:14

The smallest deed is better than the greatest intention!

A missionary was sailing home on furlough when she heard a cry one night—a cry that is perhaps the most difficult to hear when at sea: "Man overboard!" She arose quickly from her berth, lit the lamp on the bracket in her cabin, and then held the lamp at the window of her cabin in hopes of seeing some sign of life in the murky dark waters outside.

Seeing nothing she hung the lamp back on its bracket, snuffed it out, and returned to her berth with prayers for the man lost at sea. In the morning, to her surprise she discovered the man had been rescued. Not only that, but she learned it was the flash of her lamp through the porthole that showed those on deck the location of the missing man, who was clinging desperately to a rope still attached to the deck. He was pulled from the cold waters in the nick of time. Such a small deed as shining a lamp at the right time had saved a man's life.

It isn't the size of the deed you do that counts. It's the fact that you do it for good and not for evil, and with a trust that God can take every deed we perform and use it for His purposes, in our lives and in the lives of others.

Let us not love [merely] in theory or in speech but in deed and in truth [in practice and in sincerity.]

1 JOHN 3:18 AMP

I've suffered a great many
catastrophes in my life.
Most of them never happened.

A military chaplain once drew up a
"Worry Table" based upon the problems men and
women had brought to him through his years of
service. He found their worries fit into these cat-
egories:

Worries about things that never happened-
40%

Worries about past, unchangeable decisions-
30%

Worries about illness that never happened-
12%

Worries about adult children and friends
(who were able to take care of themselves)-
10%

Worries about real problems-8%

According to his chart, 92 percent of all worries are about things we can't control, concerns which are better left to God. The truth is, most of our anxieties are rooted in a failure to trust God.

We simply don't believe He is big enough or cares enough to handle our problems, give us the desires of our hearts, and keeps us—and our loved ones—from harm.

Knowing God's character, we can easily see how we worry for nothing most of the time!

God hath not given us the spirit of fear; but of power, and of love, and of a sound mind.

2 TIMOTHY 1:7

Guilt is concerned with the past. Worry is concerned about the future. Contentment enjoys the present.

*P*sychologist William Marston once asked three thousand people, "What have you to live for?" He was shocked to discover that 94 percent of the people he polled were simply enduring the present while they waited for the future. Some indicated they were waiting for "something" to happen—waiting for children to grow up and leave home, waiting for next year, waiting for another time to take a long-awaited trip, waiting for someone to die, or waiting for tomorrow. They had hope, but no ongoing purpose to their lives!

Only 6 percent of the people identified relationships and activities in the present tense of their lives that they counted as valuable reasons for living!

The 94 percent would be wise to recall the words of this poem by an unknown author:

During all the years since time began,
Today has been the friend of man; But in
his blindness and his sorrow, He looks to
yesterday and tomorrow. Forget past
trials and your sorrow. There was, but is,
no yesterday, And there may be no
tomorrow.[26]

Not that I am implying that I was in any personal want, for I have learned how to be content [satisfied to the point where I am not disturbed or disquieted] in whatever state I am.

PHILIPPIANS 4:11 AMP

People with tact have less to retract.

*B*irds sing and never have to apologize for their songs.

Dogs bark and kittens meow and never have to say, "I'm sorry for what I just said."

Lions roar and hyenas howl, but they never have to retract their statements as being untrue.

The fact is, the members of the animal kingdom are themselves, and they are true in their expression to what they were created to be.

Many times we human beings find ourselves embarrassed at our own words—feeling apologetic, caught in an awkward moment, or recognizing we have spoken the wrong words at the wrong time—because we have begun evaluating the performance of others and develop a critical attitude.

The bluejay doesn't criticize the robin. The kitten doesn't make snide remarks about the puppy. The lion doesn't ridicule the hyena. In like manner, we should not put down others whom we can never fully understand, never fully appreciate, or never fully emulate.

Stick to singing your own song today, and appreciate the uniqueness of those around you. You will easily avoid putting your foot in your mouth!

The heart of the righteous weighs its answers, but the mouth of the wicked gushes evil.

PROVERBS 15:28 NIV

*Being at peace with
yourself is a direct result
of finding peace with God.*

*T*om Dooley was a young doctor who gave up an easy career to organize hospitals and pour out his life in service to afflicted people in Southeast Asia. As he lay dying of cancer at age thirty-four, Dooley wrote to the president of Notre Dame, his alma mater:

"Dear Father Hesburgh: They've got me down. Flat on the back, with plaster, sandbags, and hot water bottles. I've contrived a way of pumping the bed up a bit so that, with a long reach, I can get to my typewriter . . . Two things prompt this note to you. The first is that whenever my cancer acts up a bit . . . I turn inward. Less do I think of my hospitals around the world, or of ninety-four doctors, fund-raisers, and the like. More do I think of one Divine Doctor and my personal fund of grace . . . I have monstrous phantoms; all men do. And inside and outside the wind blows. But when the time comes, like now, then the storm around me does not matter. The winds within me do not matter. Nothing human or earthly can touch me. A peace gathers in my heart. What seems unpossessable, I can possess. What seems unfathomable, I can fathom. What is unutterable, I can utter. Because I can pray. I can communicate. How do people endure anything on earth if they cannot have God?[27]

The peace of God, which passeth all understanding, shall keep your hearts and minds through Christ Jesus.

PHILIPPIANS 4:7

If you want to make an
easy job seem hard, just
keep putting off doing it.

When Beth's boss asked her to take on an extra project, Beth saw the opportunity to prove she could handle greater responsibility. She immediately began to think how she might approach the task, and her enthusiasm ran high. But when the time came to start the project, Beth found herself telling her boss she was too busy to do the job justice. The project was given to someone else, who earned a promotion for completing it successfully. Beth didn't receive any new opportunities and eventually took a position with another firm.

What had kept Beth from doing the project? Simple procrastination. She put off getting started on the project until she was paralyzed with fear—fear that she might not be able to do the job or that her performance would not meet her boss' expectation. In the end, Beth didn't move ahead and thus reinforced her fears with a bigger sense of insecurity about her own ability.

If you find yourself procrastinating, ask God to show you how to overcome your fear, then do what He says. He wants you to succeed and live a fulfilled life, but you must step out in faith for Him to bless you.

How long are ye slack to go to possess the land, which the LORD God of your fathers hath given you?

JOSHUA 18:3

Love sees through a
telescope not a microscope.

One Christmas morning, little Amy was delighted to find a beautiful golden-haired doll among the presents she unwrapped. "She's so pretty!" Amy squealed in excitement as she hugged her new doll. Then rushing to hug her grandmother, the giver of the doll, she cried, "Thank you, thank you, thank you!"

Amy played with her new doll most of the day, but toward evening she put it down and sought out one of her old dolls. Amy cradled the tattered and dilapidated old doll in her arms. Its hair had nearly worn away, its nose was broken, one eye was askew, and an arm was missing.

"Well, well," Grandma noted, "it seems as though you like that old dolly better."

"I like the beautiful doll you gave me, Grandma," little Amy explained, "but I love this old doll more, because if I didn't love her, no one else would."

We all know the saying, "Beauty is in the eye of the beholder." A similar saying might be, "Love is the choice of the beholder." When we see faults in others, we can choose to look beyond them. We can choose to love them regardless of their negative attributes, faults, or quirks.

Love endures long and is patient and kind . . . it takes no account of the evil done to it [it pays no attention to a suffered wrong.]

1 CORINTHIANS 13:4,5 AMP

• 235 •

*Life is not a problem to be solved,
but a gift to be enjoyed.*

*T*he fictional character Sherlock Holmes is known for his keen power of observation in solving crimes. But Holmes also used his observation skills in renewing his faith. In *The Adventure of the Naval Treaty,* Dr. Watson says of Holmes: " He walked past the couch to an open window and held up the drooping stalk of a moss rose, looking down at the dainty blend of crimson and green. It was a new phase of his character to me, for I had never before seen him show an interest in natural objects.

"'There is nothing in which deduction is so necessary as in religion,' said he, leaning with his back against the shutters. . . . 'Our highest assurance of the goodness of Providence seems to me to rest in the flowers. All other things, our powers, our desires, our food, are really necessary for our existence in the first instance. But this rose is an extra. Its smell and its color are an embellishment of life, not a condition of it. It is only goodness which gives extras, and so I say again that we have much to hope from the flowers'"[28]

Life is filled with extras—gifts from a loving God that embellish and enrich our lives. Take time to observe some of them today!

This is the day that the LORD has made; let us rejoice and be glad in it.

PSALM 118:24 NIV

*A pint of example is worth
a barrelful of advice.*

On the fourth Sunday of July, the descendants of Roberto and Raquel Beaumont celebrate "Offspring Day." They have been doing this since 1956, when Raquel gathered her five preteen children around the dinner table at their home in Lima, Peru. She placed a rose by the napkin of each daughter and a carnation by the napkin of each son.

Knowing in a few years her children would be going their separate ways, she told her children that the gifts she gave them on Offspring Day were not mere flowers, but a token of her true gift to them—time and love. Furthermore, she expected them to pass on those same gifts to their children. Through the years, Raquel was the best example of her message: she always had time and love for each of her children, who regularly sought her advice and encouragement.

On Offspring Day each year, the elders who gather offer words of wisdom to their children. The young are encouraged to pick one thing about themselves they hope to improve in the coming year. It is a time for the generations to hear from one another and to set new goals for relationships. They do it all in the spirit of "Raquel's example."

Brethren, join in following my example, and observe those who walk according to the pattern you have in us.

PHILIPPIANS 3:17 NASB

• 239 •

Beware lest your footprints
on the sand of time leave
only the marks of a heel.

*I*n *Grand Essentials,* Ben Patterson writes:
"I have a theory about old age. . . . I believe that
when life has whittled us down, when joints have
failed and skin has wrinkled . . . what is left of us
will be what we were all along, in our essence.

"Exhibit A is a distant uncle. . . . All his life
he did nothing but find new ways to get rich. . . .
He spent his senescence very comfortably, drool-
ing and babbling constantly about the money he
had made. . . . When life whittled him down to
his essence, all there was left was raw greed.

"Exhibit B is my wife's grandmother. . . . The
best example I can think of was when we asked
her to pray before dinner. She would reach out
and hold the hands of those sitting beside her, a
broad, beatific smile would spread across her

face, her dim eyes would fill with tears as she looked up to heaven, and her chin would quaver as she poured out her love to Jesus. That was Edna in a nutshell. She loved Jesus and she love people. She couldn't remember our names, but she couldn't keep her hands from patting us lovingly whenever we got near her. When life whittled her down to her essence, all there was left was love: love for God and love for people."[29]

*The memory of the righteous
will be a blessing, but the
name of the wicked will rot.*

PROVERBS 10:7 NIV

If you were given a nickname descriptive of your character, would you be proud of it?

*I*n 1955 the city buses in Montgomery, Alabama, were segregated by law. White people and black people were not allowed to sit together.

On December 1 of that year, Mrs. Rosa Parks was riding the bus home from her job at a tailor shop. As the section for whites filled up, the black people were ordered to move to the back to make room for the white passengers who were boarding. Three blacks in Mrs. Parks' row moved, but Mrs. Parks remained in her seat. Later she said, "our mistreatment was just not right, and I was tired of it. I knew someone had to take the first step. So I made up my mind not to move."

The bus driver asked her if she was going to stand up. "No, I am not," she answered him. Mrs. Parks was arrested and taken to jail. Four days later black people and white sympathizers organized a boycott of the city bus line that lasted until a year later, when the Supreme Court declared the segregated-bus ordinance unconstitutional.

Mrs. Parks is known today as the "mother of the modern-day civil rights movement." Her name inspires others to be courageous and do what is right, despite the circumstances.

*A good name is rather to
be chosen than great riches.*

PROVERBS 22:1

*It's easy to identify people
who can't count to ten.
They're in front of you in the
supermarket express lane.*

A woman once visited a friend in
Cambridge, Massachusetts, home of several well-
known institutions of higher learning. She
accompanied the friend to a supermarket on
Saturday afternoon, finding it crammed with
shoppers and very long checkout lines.

While the two of them stood patiently in line,
they noticed a college-age young man wheel a
filled shopping cart into the cash register stall
that was clearly marked, "Express Line—8 Items
Or Less."

The checkout girl of the express line looked
at the loaded cart and then at the young man. He

was trying to ignore her exasperated expression by fumbling for his checkbook in his knapsack.

Realizing she was stuck with a stubborn and inconsiderate customer, the girl said loudly to the high school student who was helping her bag groceries, "This guy either goes to Harvard and can't count, or he goes to M.I.T. and can't read!"

Although we don't always think of it in these terms, impatience reveals a selfish and often mean spirit, while patience is really an act of kindness.

Be patient with everyone.

1 THESSALONIANS 5:14 NIV

• 245 •

Tact is the art of making a point without making an enemy.

In looking over a café menu, a woman noticed that both a chicken salad sandwich and a chicken sandwich were listed. She decided to order the chicken salad sandwich, but absent-mindedly wrote "chicken sandwich" on her order slip. When the waiter brought the chicken sandwich, she protested immediately, insisting the waiter had erred.

Most waiters would have picked up the order slip and shown the customer the mistake she had made. But instead he expressed regret at the error, picked up the sandwich, returned to the kitchen, and a moment later placed a chicken salad sandwich in front of the woman.

While eating her sandwich, the woman picked up her order slip and noticed the mistake she had made. When it was time to pay for the meal, she apologized to the waiter and offered to pay for both sandwiches. The waiter said, "No, Ma'am. That's perfectly all right. I'm just happy you've forgiven me for being right."

Reckless words pierce like a sword, but the tongue of the wise brings healing.

PROVERBS 12:18 NIV

Silence is one of the hardest arguments to refute.

Ruth Bell Graham tells a humorous story about her daughters, Anne and Bunny. When Ruth ran to the kitchen to investigate some loud cries, she found three-year-old Bunny holding her hand to her cheek, looking very disapprovingly at her sister. "Mommy," explained five-year-old Anne, "I'm teaching Bunny the Bible. I'm slapping her on one cheek and teaching her to turn the other one so I can slap it too."[30]

When we are wronged, our first response is more likely to fight back than to turn the other cheek. But many have found that fighting back can be counterproductive.

Missionary E. Stanley Jones was being publicly slandered by someone he had once helped. Jones' first response was to write his accuser a letter he relates was "the kind of reply you are proud of the first five minutes, the second five minutes you're not so certain, and the third five minutes you know you're wrong."

Jones knew his comments would win the argument, but lose the person. "The Christian," he said, "is not in the business of winning arguments, but of winning people," and he tore up the letter. A few weeks later—without having said a word—Jones received a letter of apology from the one who had turned on him.

Whoso keepeth his mouth and his tongue keepeth his soul from troubles.

PROVERBS 21:23

The best antique is an old friend.

A woman was in a serious automobile accident in a city far from home. She felt so enclosed in a cocoon of pain, she didn't realize how lonely she was until a "forgotten" friend in the city came to visit her. She firmly but gently said to her, "you should not be alone."

In the weeks that followed, this friend's advice rang in the injured woman's ears and helped her to overcome her otherwise reserved nature. When another friend called from a city several hundred miles away to say she wanted to come stay with her, the injured woman didn't say, "Don't bother"—as would have been her normal response. Rather, she said, "Please come." The friend was a wonderful encourager and nurse to her, reading the Psalms aloud when she was still too weak to read herself. Then yet another friend offered to come and help in her recovery. Again she swallowed her pride and said, "Please do." This friend stayed for several months until the injured woman was able to care for herself.

Even Jesus did not carry His own cross all the way to Calvary. He allowed another to help shoulder His burden. It's all right to ask for help and to receive help. You don't have to "go it alone." Let a friend help you.

Your own friend and your father's friend, forsake not . . . Better is a neighbor who is near [in spirit] than a brother who is far off [in heart].

PROVERBS 27:10 AMP

If you can't feed a hundred people then just feed one.

When thirteen-year-old Bobby Hill, the son of a U.S. Army sergeant stationed in Italy, read a book about the work of Nobel Prize winner Albert Schweitzer, he decided to do something to help the medical missionary. He sent a bottle of aspirin to Lieutenant General Richard C. Lindsay, Commander of the Allied air forces in Southern Europe, asking if any of his airplanes could parachute the bottle of aspirin to Dr. Schweitzer's jungle hospital in Africa.

Upon hearing the letter, an Italian radio station issued an appeal, resulting in more than $400,000 worth of donated medical supplies. The French and Italian governments each supplied a plane to fly the medicines and the boy to Dr. Schweitzer. The grateful doctor responded,

"I never thought a child could do so much for my hospital."

None of us may be able to solve all the problems in the world, but we can feed a hungry family in a nearby neighborhood, clothe the homeless person who has just arrived at a shelter, or give a blanket to a street person who lives near our office building. If every person who could offer help would take just one step every month to meet just one person's need, think what might be accomplished!

As we have therefore opportunity,
let us do good unto all men.

GALATIANS 6:10

• 253 •

*The trouble with stretching
the truth is that
it's apt to snap back.*

A Sunday school teacher once told her
adult class, "Next Sunday I am going to teach a
very important lesson. I want you all to read
Chapter 17 of St. Mark's Gospel in anticipation
of it." The members of the class nodded, indicating a willingness to do as the teacher requested.

The following Sunday the teacher asked the
class, "Those who read Chapter 17 of St. Mark's
Gospel during this past week, please raise your
hands." Nearly all the people in the room raised
their hands.

The teacher then said, "That's very interesting. The Gospel of Mark had only sixteen chap-
ters. But at least I know that my lesson is going
to hit its mark. Today I'm going to teach what
Jesus had to say about lying."

Perhaps the greatest punishment for lying is not that a person gets caught in the lie, but rather, the "hidden" punishment that a liar can never truly believe what anyone else says.

Tell the truth! You'll suffer far less embarrassment and be much healthier emotionally. Even if truth-telling brings temporary pain, God will honor your courage and bless you for doing the right thing.

A false witness shall not be unpunished, and he that speaketh lies shall not escape.

PROVERBS 19:5

Birthdays are good for you.
Statistics show that
the people who have the
most live the longest.

*T*here once was a woman who, upon seeing her hair turn gray, decided she must be getting old. She immediately slowed her pace, refused to wear bright colors, tried to act more sedated, and began to wear "sensible shoes." She let her hair grow long and put it up in a bun on her head, wore long sleeves to cover what she was sure must be unsightly "old lady" arms, and could often be heard telling friends who asked how she was doing, "I suppose I'm doing as well as could expected for a person my age."

One day she overheard a teenager ask a friend, "How old is Miss Tilly?" The friend said, "Well, from the way she looks and acts, I'd say she's at least 65 or 70." The woman was shocked—they were talking about her, and she was only 55! She decided she was looking far too old for her years and immediately shifted into reverse. Bright colors, high heels, and more stylish clothes rejoined her closet. She cut her hair and used a rinse to color the gray. Several months later, a 48-year-old man asked her out and wouldn't believe her when she told him her age.

She concluded, "Fifty-five is a better speed limit than age limit."

So teach us to number our days, that we may apply our hearts unto wisdom.

PSALM 90:12

Faults are thick where love is thin.

*H*ave you ever noticed:

When others are set in their ways, they're obstinate, but you are firm and resolved.

When your neighbor doesn't like your friend, she's prejudiced, but when you don't like her friend, you're a good judge of human nature.

When she tries to treat someone especially well, she's buttering up the person, but when you do so, you're being thoughtful.

When she takes time to do things well, she's lazy, but when you do so, you're meticulous.

When she spends a lot, she's a spendthrift, but when you overdo, you're generous.

When she picks flaws in things, she's critical, but when you do, you are perceptive.

When she is mild-mannered, you call her weak, but when you are, you're gracious.

When she dresses well, she is extravagant, but when you do, you're tastefully in style.

When she says what she thinks, she's spiteful, but when you do, you're being honest.

When she takes great risks, she's foolhardy, but when you do, you're brave.

Above all things have fervent charity among yourselves: for charity shall cover the multitude of sins.

I Peter 4:8

The only way to have
a friend is to be one.

$\mathcal{A}$ young family in the 1950s had just purchased their first television set. All the neighbors gathered to help them put up the antenna on the roof of their home. Since they had only the simplest of tools, they weren't making much progress.

Then a new neighbor and his wife showed up with a large, elaborate tool box, filled with just about any gadget or tool one could imagine. They had everything needed to install the antenna, which was up in near record time after their arrival.

The group of volunteers immediately went inside to see what kind of reception their neighbors would get on their new television set. The picture was crystal clear! Success was theirs!

As the neighbors stood around congratulating themselves on their fine work, they thanked their new neighbors for their valuable assistance. One of the women asked, "What is it that you make with such a well-equipped tool box?"

The new neighbors smiled sincerely and replied with genuine warmth, "Friends."

A man that hath friends
must shew himself friendly.

PROVERBS 18:24

The world wants your best
but God wants your all.

*J*anette Oak, best-selling novelist with more than forty books to her credit, is considered the modern "pioneer author" for Christian fiction. Hew books have sold millions of copies since her first novel was published in 1979.

When she first decided to write, she said to God, "Lord, I'm going to write this book. If it works, and if I discover I have talent, I'll give it all to You."

Janette sensed God was not pleased with the bargain she was trying to strike with Him. She felt in her heart as if He were responding, "If you're serious about this, then I want everything before you start." Thus she gave Him her ambitions and dreams, and trusted Him to teach her, whether she was successful or not.

Out of that resolve came a second resolve. She refused to compromise her principles. Although she would write realistically, her stories would be "wholesome and good and encouraging." Many thought that approach was doomed to failure at the outset, but a shelf of novels later . . . Janette Oak has proven "God can teach spiritual truths through fictional characters."[31]

Thou shalt love the Lord thy God with all thy heart, and with all thy soul, and with all thy mind.

MATTHEW 22:37

Hindsight explains the injury that foresight would have prevented.

The mother of six children walked into her house one day to see all her children huddled together in a circle. She approached them to see what had evoked such intense interest, and she could hardly believe her eyes.

To her horror, in the middle of the circle of children were several baby skunks. She immediately screamed at the top of her voice, "Children! Run, run, run! Out, out, out!"

At the sound of their mother's alarmed voice, each child quickly grabbed a baby skunk and headed for the door. The screaming and panic, of course, set off the instinctual danger alarm in the skunks, and each of them quickly dispelled its horrible scent. Each child and the house itself were doused with an aroma that lingered for weeks, regardless of intense scrubbing and use of disinfectants.

How we react has greater negative consequences than the initial negative situation we encounter! Don't make matters worse by unplanned, emotion-driven, spur-of-the-moment behavior. Choose to act rather than to react, taking sufficient time to select a course of action based upon calm reason and thoughtful prayer.

Do not forsake wisdom, and she will protect you . . . When you walk, your steps will not be hampered; when you run, you will not stumble.

PROVERBS 4:6,12 NIV

*Do not in the darkness
of night, what you'd
shun in broad daylight.*

*H*erbert V. Prochnow has constructed a ten-part "Character Quiz"—an interesting checkup as to just how much we might choose to be "children of light":

1. If you found a wallet with $1,000, would you give it to the owner if no one knew you found it?

2. If you could advance yourself unfairly, would you do it if no one would ever find out?

3. If the bus driver failed to collect your fare, would you voluntarily pay it?

4. If there were no locks on any house, store, or bank, would you take anything if no one found out?

5. If your business partner died, would you pay his relatives their fair share, if you didn't have to?

6. If you were an employer, would you hire yourself at your salary?

7. If you were an employer, would you like to be working for yourself?

8. If you are a parent, would you like to be the child of a parent like you?

9. If you had a choice, would you like to live in a community with people working in church, civic, and community affairs like you do?

10. If you had to live with someone just like you for the rest of your life, would you count it a privilege?[32]

The night is far spent, the day is at hand: let us therefore cast off the works of darkness, and let us put on the armour of light.

ROMANS 13:12

*I am defeated, and know it,
if I meet any human being
from whom I find myself
unable to learn anything.*

Carlos Romulo, the former president of the
Philippines, won an oratorical contest in the
Manila high school he attended as a young man.
His father was puzzled, however, when he saw his
son ignore the congratulations of one of the
other contestants. As they left the auditorium he
asked, "Why didn't you shake hands with Julio?"

Carlos said, "I have no use for Julio. He was
speaking ill of me before the contest." The father
put his arm around his son and said, "Your
grandfather used to tell me that the taller the
bamboo grows, the lower it bends. Remember
that always, my boy. The taller the bamboo
grows, the lower it bends."

Every person has something to teach us—not only those who are experts in their fields or tell us what we want to hear. Each person is a living encyclopedia of ideas, insights, facts, experiences, and opinions.

A woman once advised a new employee: "Fifty percent of the people in this organization will teach you what to do and the other 50 percent what not to do. It's your challenge to figure out which percent goes with which person." Even if a person doesn't have a good example for you to follow, you can always learn from him or her what not to do!

A wise man will hear, and will increase learning; and a man of understanding shall attain unto wise counsels.

PROVERBS 1:5

*Honesty is the first chapter
of the book of wisdom.*

The editor of the "weddings and engagement" section of a small-town newspaper grew tired of hearing from the town's citizens that she always embellished her reports of parties and celebrations. She decided that in the next issue she was going to tell the truth and see if she had greater favor with the citizenry. She wrote the following item:

"Married—Miss Sylvan Rhodes and James Collins, last Saturday at the Baptist parsonage, by the Rev. J. Gordon. The bride is a very ordinary town girl, who doesn't know any more about cooking than a jackrabbit and never helped her mother three days in her life. She is not a beauty by any means and has a gait like a duck. The groom is an up-to-date loafer. He has been living off the old folks at home all his life and is now worth shucks. It will be a hard life."

We may not always need to be so brutally "honest" in telling the truth! Truth, after all, is ultimately known only by God—who alone has the ability to see into the hearts of men and women and know everything involved in any situation or relationship. Rather, we should be honest in expressing our hopes for another person's best welfare and success. That is a truth everybody loves to hear.

*Provide things honest in
the sight of all men.*

ROMANS 12:17

God always gives His best to those who leave the choice with Him.

*A*uthor Elizabeth Elliot writes in *A Lamp for My Feet* about a game she played as a young girl. She writes, "My mother or father would say, 'Shut your eyes and hold out your hand.' That was the promise of some lovely surprise. I trusted them, so I shut my eyes instantly and held out my hand. Whatever they were going to give me I was ready to take." She continues, "So should it be in our trust of our heavenly Father. Faith is the willingness to receive whatever He wants to give, or the willingness not to have what He does not want to give."[33]

If your prayers aren't answered in the way you expect them to be, there may be a good reason! Several months before Christmas, Jared begged his mother to buy him a new bicycle just like his friend's—and he had to have it now. His mother was a single mom, however, and there was no extra money for a new bicycle until Christmas.

Jared's friend generously lent him his bicycle to ride, and the longer Jared rode it, the more he realized it really wasn't the right bicycle for him. For one thing, it didn't have the racing brakes he wanted.

How often do we think God has forgotten us, when He's merely giving us time to understand what we really want and bringing us His best?

Blessed be the Lord, who daily
loadeth us with benefits,
even the God of our salvation.

PSALM 68:19

A lot of people mistake
a short memory
for a clear conscience.

*I*n the 1890s a man drove by the farm of Mrs. John R. McDonald. A sudden gust of wind caught his black derby hat and whirled it onto the McDonald property. He searched in vain for the hat and finally drove off bareheaded.

Mrs. McDonald retrieved the hat, and for the next forty-five years various members of her family wore it. Finally the old derby was beyond repair, completely worn out. It was at that point Mrs. McDonald went to the local newspaper and advertised for the owner of the hat. She noted in her ad that while the hat had been on the *heads* of the menfolk in her family, the hat had been on her *conscience* for forty-five years!

Is something nagging at your heart today— an awareness that you have committed a wrong against another person or a feeling that something has gone amiss in a relationship? Don't "stuff" those feelings. Seek to make amends. The sooner you do, the easier you'll find the reconciliation of restoration—and the easier you'll find your rest at night.

A guilty conscience is a very heavy load to carry through life—one for which Jesus died on the cross. He did His part. Now you do yours and obtain the freedom and peace He purchased for you!

Herein do I exercise myself, to have always a conscience void of offense toward God, and toward men.

ACTS 24:16

*Faith is not belief without proof,
but trust without reservation.*

*D*uring the terrible days of the Blitz in
World War II, a father—holding his young
daughter by the hand—ran from a building that
had been struck by a bomb. In the front yard was
a large hole left by a shell explosion several days
before. Seeking shelter as quickly as possible, the
father jumped into the hole and then held up his
arms for his young daughter to follow.

Terrified at the explosions around her and
unable to see her father in the darkness of the
hole, she cried, "I can't see you, Papa!"

The father looked up against the sky that was
lit with white tracer lights and tinted red by
burning buildings and called to his daughter,
who was standing in silhouette at the hole's edge,
"But I can see you, my darling. Jump!"

The little girl jumped . . . not because she could see her father, but because she trusted him to tell her the truth and to do what was best for her.

We may not be able to discern clearly where it is our Heavenly Father is leading us, but we can trust it is to a good place. We may not know what God has "up His sleeve," but we can trust His arms to be everlasting.

I know whom I have believed,
and am persuaded that he is able to
keep that which I have committed
unto him against that day.

2 TIMOTHY 1:12

A day hemmed in prayer
is less likely to unravel.

*I*t was 2 A.M. when a weary traveler landed in Tahiti. Her flight from Hawaii had been a turbulent one, causing a delay in her arrival on the island. The stormy skies had also forced her connecting flight to a nearby island to be cancelled, forcing her to make plans to spend at least a day near the airport. An hour later, she found herself standing with her luggage in a small but clean motel room, totally exhausted after more than twenty-four hours of travel. Her mind, however, refused to stop racing with concern about whom to call and what to do.

The woman was on a short-term missionary trip to help set up a clinic on a remote South Seas island. Now she was beginning to wonder if she had heard God correctly! At that hour, and as weary as she was, she felt alone at the edge of the world. Glancing down at her watch, she saw it read 11 A.M.—the time her Bible Study group had said they would be in prayer for her. *They're praying right now!* she thought, and suddenly, she felt deep peace and comfort. Within minutes, she was sound asleep.

When you are feeling as if you are about to unravel inside, turn to prayer. The travel route of prayer is never misdirected or put off schedule— nor is it dangerous! On the contrary, prayer gives peace and helps us avoid danger.

Pray about everything; tell God your needs and don't forget to thank him for his answers. If you do this, you will experience God's peace . . . His peace will keep your thoughts and your hearts quiet and at rest.

PHILIPPIANS 4:6,7 TLB

When you flee temptations don't leave a forwarding address.

Sally was trying desperately to save all the pennies she could for the doll carriage she wanted to buy. She was turning in aluminum cans, offering to do extra chores . . . anything to make a few more cents a week.

One night as she was saying her bedtime prayers, her mother overheard Sally say in great earnest, "O Lord, please help me to save my money for the doll carriage in Mr. Brown's store window. It's so beautiful, and I want it so much. It's just right for my doll. And I'd be sure to let my friends play with it too."

Pleased by her daughter's prayer, Sally's mother was startled to hear the final line of the prayer. "And please God, don't let the ice cream man come down our street this week!"

Just as we are each unique in our talents, abilities, background, and experiences, we are also unique in what tempts us. What is tempting to one person may not be at all tempting to another.

Although the enemy of our souls knows our weak points, we know our Strength—Jesus. As we stick close to Him, when temptation comes, we can draw on His strength to turn from it.

Always say yes to Jesus, and saying no to temptation will become easy!

Now flee from youthful lusts, and pursue righteousness, faith, love and peace, with those who call on the Lord from a pure heart.

2 TIMOTHY 2:22 NASB

*A coincidence is a small
miracle where God prefers
to remain anonymous.*

*V*ictor Frankl was stripped of everything
he owned when he was arrested by the Nazis in
World War II. He arrived at Auschwitz with only
his manuscript—a book he had been researching
and writing for years—sewn into the lining of his
coat. Upon arrival, even that was taken from him.
He later wrote, "I had to undergo and overcome
the loss of my spiritual child. . . . It seemed as if
nothing and no one would survive me. I found
myself confronted with the question of whether
under such circumstances my life was ultimately
void of any meaning."

Days later, the Nazis forced the prisoners to
give up their clothes. In return Frankl was given
rags of an inmate who had been sent to the gas
chamber. In the pocket of the garment he found

a torn piece of paper—a page from a Hebrew prayer book. On it was the foremost Jewish prayer, "Shema Yisrael" which begins, "Hear, O Israel! The Lord our God is one God."

Frankl says, "How should I have interpreted such a 'coincidence' other than as a challenge to live my thoughts instead of merely putting them on paper?" He later wrote in his classic masterpiece, *Man's Search for Meaning,* "He who has a why to live for can bear almost any how."[34]

Who can put into words and tell the mighty deeds of the Lord? Or can show forth all the praise [that is due Him]?

PSALM 106:2 AMP

Sometimes the Lord calms the storm; sometimes He lets the storm rage and calms His child.

*I*n *Especially for a Woman,* Beverly LaHaye writes about how upset she was when her husband, Tim, told her he wanted to take flying lessons. Her quick response was, "I think you're foolish! Why would you want to get into a plane with only one engine?"

Tim asked her to pray about the matter, but she writes, "I started right off giving God my opinions and drawing my own conclusions. My fear . . . was controlling me." Tim suggested, "Be open with the Lord. . . . Let Him know you're afraid of flying, but that you're willing to be changed if that's what He would have."

Beverly did just that. Tim took flying lessons, and repeatedly she committed her fears—and their lives—to the Lord.

Years later she was a passenger in a commuter plane that was caught in a storm. As the plane bounced in the sky, the LaHaye's attorney—normally a very calm man—felt sure they were going to crash. Then he looked over and saw that Beverly was asleep! He asked her later, "How could you sleep so peacefully?"

Beverly responded, "It has to be God. Only He could have brought me from that crippling fearfulness . . . to a place where I could fly through such a storm and be at peace."[35]

The peace of God, which transcends all understanding, will guard your hearts and your minds in Christ Jesus.

PHILIPPIANS 4:7 NIV

*The past should be a springboard
not a hammock.*

Many people are good starters but poor
finishers. When the going starts getting tough
they listen to the little imp on their shoulder that
whispers, "You can't do it" and "You'll never
make it." Many others do not even start.

What we must realize is that while "doing
something: requires a risk, so does "doing
nothing." The risk of action may be failure, but
the risks of a failure to act can be stagnation, dis-
satisfaction, and frustration . . . even loss to an
evil enemy.

The story of the covered wagon crossing the
plains toward the Golden West began with a song:

The Coward never started;
The Weak died on the way;
Only the Strong came through!

That's the way it is in life. But strength does not refer only to physical strength. True strength flows from the strong spirit—a spirit made powerful by a close relationship with God. He gives us the will to succeed, the dreams that will not die, and the wisdom to turn any evil into a blessing.

Lean on God for direction, and keep leaning on Him for the wisdom and courage to finish what you begin!

This one thing I do, forgetting those things which are behind, and reaching forth unto those things which are before.

PHILIPPIANS 3:13

The teacher asked the pupils to tell the meaning of lovingkindness. A little boy jumped up and said, "Well, if I was hungry and someone gave me a piece of bread that would be kindness. But if they put a little jelly on it, that would be lovingkindness."

*K*indness provides a house, but love makes a home.

Kindness packs an adequate sack lunch, but love puts a note of encouragement inside.

Kindness provides a television set or computer as a learning aid, but love controls the remote control and cares enough to insist a child "sign off."

Kindness sends a child to bed on time, but love tucks the covers around a child's neck and provides a goodnight hug and kiss.

Kindness cooks a meal, but love selects the "your favorite foods" menu and lights the candles.

Kindness writes a thank-you note, but love thinks to include a joke or photograph or bookmark inside the envelope.

Kindness keeps a clean and tidy house, but love adds a bouquet of fresh flowers.

Kindness pours a glass of milk, but love occasionally adds a little chocolate sauce.

Kindness is doing what is decent, basic, courteous, and necessary for an even, smooth, and gentle flow of life.

Love is taking the extra step to make life truly exciting, creative, and meaningful. Love is what makes things *special.*

Bless the Lord, O my soul . . . who crowneth thee with lovingkindness and tender mercies; Who satisfieth thy mouth with good things.

PSALM 103:1,4,5

Laughter is a tranquilizer
with no side effects.

Norman Cousins was once asked by a group of physicians to meet with cancer patients at a veteran's hospital. He told how he had lost a quarter in a pay phone. "Operator," he said, "I put in a quarter and didn't get my number." She said, "Sir, if you give me your name and address, we'll mail the coin to you."

He recited a full and long litany of all the steps and procedures and expense involved in returning his coin that way and concluded, "Now, operator, why don't you just return my coin and let's be friends?"

She repeated her offer and then asked if he had pushed the coin-return plunger. He hadn't, but when he did, the phone box spewed out close to four dollars worth of change!

The operator said, "Sir, will you please put the coins back in the box?" Cousins replied, "If you give me your name and address I will be glad to mail you the coins."

The veterans exploded with cheers as Cousins told his story. Then one of the physicians asked, "How many of you came into this room in pain?" More than half raised their hands. "How many of you in the past few minutes had less or no pain?" All nodded "yes."

Laughter—it's one of the best pain medications ever!

A merry heart doeth good like a medicine.

PROVERBS 17:22

God never asks about our ability or our inability— just our availability.

One of the items in *Ripley's Believe It or Not* is a picture of a plain bar of iron. It is valued at $5. The same bar of iron has a far different value, however, if it is fashioned into different items.

- As a pair of horse shoes, it would be worth $50.
- As sewing needles, it would be worth $5,000.
- As balance springs for fine Swiss watches, it would be worth $500,000.

The raw material is not what is important. What's important is how raw material is developed.

Each of us has been given talents and abilities—some have received more, others less, but all have received something as a unique gift from

God. As Christians, we also enjoy spiritual gifts which flow from the Holy Spirit of God.

The value of these raw materials, however, is a moot point unless we develop and use our talents, abilities, and spiritual gifts as a force for divine good in this world.

If you don't know what your abilities and gifts are, ask God to reveal them to you. Then ask Him to show you what He wants you to do with them. Your happiness and success in life will be found in fulfilling His plan for your life.

I heard the voice of the Lord, saying, Whom shall I send, and who will go for us? Then said I, Here am I; send me.

ISAIAH 6:8

• 293 •

Whether you think you can or think you can't, you're right.

$\mathcal{A}$ new prison was built in British Columbia to replace the old Fort Alcan prison that had been used to house inmates for hundreds of years. After the prisoners were moved into their new quarters, they became part of a work crew to strip the old prison of lumber, electrical appliances, and plumbing that might be reused. Under the supervision of guards, the inmates began tearing down the old prison walls.

As they did, they were shocked at what they found. Although massive locks had sealed heavy metal doors and two-inch steel bars had covered the windows of the cells, the walls of the prison had actually been made out of paper and clay, painted to resemble iron! If any of the prisoners had given a mighty heave or hard kick against a wall, they might easily have knocked a hole in it, allowing for escape. For years, however, they had huddled in their locked cells, regarding escape as impossible.

Nobody had ever tried to escape because they thought it was impossible.

Many people today are prisoners of fear. They never attempt to pursue their dreams because the thought of reaching them seems impossible. How do you know you can't succeed if you don't try?

As he thinketh in his heart, so is he.

PROVERBS 23:7

*The best way to cheer yourself up
is to cheer up somebody else.*

*T*he grief-stricken mother sat in a hospital room in stunned silence, tears streaming down her cheeks. She had just lost her only child. She gazed into space as the head nurse asked her, "Did you notice the little boy sitting in the hall just outside?" The woman shook her head no.

The nurse continued. "His mother was brought here by ambulance from their poor one-room apartment. The two of them came to this country only three months ago, because all their family members had been killed in war. They don't know anyone here.

"That little boy has been sitting outside his mother's room every day for a week in hopes his mother would come out of her coma and speak to him."

By now the woman was listening intently as the nurse continued, "Fifteen minutes ago his mother died. It's my job to tell him that, at age seven, he is all alone in the world—there's nobody who even knows his name." The nurse paused and then asked, "I don't suppose you would tell him for me?" The woman stood, dried her tears, and went out to the boy.

She put her arms around the homeless child. She invited him to come with her to her childless home. In the darkest hour of both their lives, they became lights to each other.

Give, and it shall be given unto you.

LUKE 6:38

• 297 •

Failure is not falling down.
It's staying down.

*I*n 1991 Anne Busquet was General Manager of the Optima Card division for American Express. When five of her two thousand employees were found to have hidden $24 million in losses, she was held accountable. Busquet had to face the fact that, as an intense perfectionist, she apparently came across as intimidating and confrontational to her subordinates—to the point they were more willing to lie than to report bad news to her!

Busquet lost her Optima job, but was given a second chance by American Express: an opportunity to salvage one of its smaller businesses. Her self-esteem shaken, she nearly turned down the offer. Then she decided this was her chance to alter the way she related to others. She took on the new job as a personal challenge to change.

Realizing she had to be much more under-standing, she began to work on being more patient and listening more carefully and intently. She learned to solicit bad news in an unintimi-dating way.

Four years after she was removed from her pre-vious position, Ann Busquet was promoted to be an executive vice-president at American Express.

Failure is not the end; it is a teacher for a new beginning and a better life.

A just man falleth seven times,
and riseth up again.

PROVERBS 24:16

• 299 •

The difference between genius and stupidity is that genius has its limits.

A partially deaf boy trudged into his home one day after school. In his hand, he carried a note. It was a note from school officials, suggesting that his parents remove him from school. According to those wise officials, this boy was "too stupid to learn."

Upon reading the note, the boy's mother vowed, "My son Tom isn't too stupid to learn. I'll teach him myself." And that is exactly what she did.

Many years later when Tom died, many Americans paid tribute to him by turning off their lights for one full minute. This was a fitting tribute, for Tom Edison invented the light bulb— along with motion pictures and the phonograph. In all, he was credited with more than a thousand patents. He also had a gift for powerful, motivating words. You will read several of his quotes in this book.

Neither you nor anyone you work with is beyond learning. No one is beyond discovering new ways to express talent, enthusiasm, creativity, and love. No one is beyond receiving affection and encouragement.

Never give up on yourself, no matter what anyone else says. Stand up for others, and encourage them to stay the course as well. Your Heavenly Father hasn't given up on any of you. And He never will.

We are God's workmanship, created in Christ Jesus to do good works, which God prepared in advance for us to do.

EPHESIANS 2:10 NIV

The best way to make workers miserable is to satisfy all of their demands.

*I*n *Little Women,* Mrs. March tells this story to her daughters:

Once upon a time, there were four girls who had enough to eat and drink and wear, a good many comforts and pleasures, kind friends and parents—and yet they were not content, always wishing for something more. Finally they asked an old woman for advice. "When you feel discontented," she told them, "think over your blessings, and be grateful."

They decided to try her advice and were surprised to see how well off they were. One girl discovered money couldn't keep shame and sorrow out of rich people's houses. Another learned she was a great deal happier with her youth, health, and good spirits than a certain fretful, feeble old lady who couldn't enjoy her comforts. The third found that, disagreeable as it was to help get dinner, it was harder still to have to go begging for it. The fourth girl learned that even carnelian rings were not so valuable as good behavior. So they agreed to stop complaining and to enjoy the blessings they already possessed.

Wanting something does not mean it's best for us. If you want to be content, learn to be grateful for what you have.

Be content with what you have.

HEBREWS 13:5 NIV

Our greatest danger in life is in permitting the urgent things to crowd out the important.

A time-management expert addressed a group of business students. He pulled out a one-gallon Mason jar and set it on the table. Then he produced a dozen fist-sized rocks and carefully placed them into the jar. Then he asked, "Is this jar full?"

Everyone said yes. Then he reached under the table and pulled out a bucket of gravel. He dumped it in and shook the jar. He asked the group again, "Is the jar full?"

By this time the class was on to him. "Probably not," one student answered. Then the instructor reached under the table and grabbed a bucket of sand. He dumped the sand, which went into all of the spaces between the rocks and the gravel. He asked, "Is this jar full?"

"No!" the class shouted.

Next, he grabbed a pitcher of water and began to pour it in until the jar was filled to the brim. "What is the point of this illustration?" he asked.

One student offered, "No matter how full your schedule is, you can always fit some more things in it!"

"No," the speaker replied, "the truth this illustration teaches us is: if you don't put the big rocks in first, you'll never get them in."

Ask yourself, "What are the 'big rocks' in my life?" Put those in your jar first.

"Where your treasure is,
there your heart will be also."

MATTHEW 6:21 NIV

Nobody can make you feel inferior without your consent.

*T*hree women on a hike came upon an unlocked cabin deep in the woods. Receiving no response to their knocks, they went inside to find one room, simply furnished. Nothing seemed unusual except that the large, potbellied, cast iron stove was hung from the ceiling, suspended in midair by wires.

The psychologist said, "It is obvious this lonely trapper has elevated his stove so he can curl up under it and experience a return to the womb." The engineer responded, "Nonsense! This is thermo-dynamics! He has found a way to distribute heat more evenly in his cabin." The theologian interrupted, "I'm sure this has religious meaning. Fire 'lifted up' has been a religious symbol for millennia."

As the three debated, the cabin owner returned. The hikers immediately asked him why the stove was hung by wires from the ceiling. He replied succinctly, "I had plenty of wire, but not much stove pipe."

Others may try to second-guess your motives, downplay your ideas, or insult you, but only you know why you do what you do, what you think and feel, and how you relate to God.

Stay true to who you are in Christ Jesus!

I am fearfully and wonderfully made.

PSALM 139:14

Do a good deed; meet a need.

*O*nce, a young orphan girl, despondent and lonely, walked through a meadow and saw a small butterfly caught in a thorn bush. The more the butterfly struggled to free itself, the deeper the thorns cut into its fragile body.

Filled with compassion, the girl released the butterfly. But, instead of flying away, the butterfly transformed into an angel and said gently, "To reward you for your kindness, I will do whatever you would like."

The girl thought for a moment, then replied, "I want to be happy!"

"Very well," the angel said. Then the heavenly creature leaned close to the girl and whispered something in her ear.

Many years later, as the orphan lay on her deathbed after a full and happy life, her friends gathered around her. "Won't you tell us your secret now," they pleaded. With a labored smile, the woman answered, "An angel told me that no matter where I went in life, I would find people who needed me—people rich or poor, young or old, meek or self-assured—and meeting those needs would bring me happiness and satisfaction."

Somewhere in your life there is someone who needs you. Are you willing to be an angel and meet that need?

Be devoted to one another in brotherly love. Honor one another above yourselves.

ROMANS 12:10 NIV

*To earn honor is better
than earning honors.*

*T*ension hung in the air. Rosalie Elliott had spelled her way to the fourth round of a national spelling bee in Washington, D.C. The eleven-year-old from South Carolina now faced the task of spelling the word "avowal." In her soft southern drawl, she began to recite the letters.

However, when she reached the next to last letter, the judges couldn't discern whether she said "a" or "e." They debated among themselves for several minutes, listening to a tape of Rosalie's effort. The crucial letter, though, was simply too accent-distorted to decipher. Finally, the lead judge sought input from the only person who could provide the answer.

"Was that second to last letter an 'a' or an 'e'?" he asked Rosalie. By this time, thanks to the whispering of her near-by competitors, Rosalie knew the correct spelling. Still, without hesitating, she replied that she had misspelled the word and walked from the stage.

The entire audience—including some fifty newspaper reporters—stood and applauded. The moment was especially proud for her parents. Out of defeat, Rosalie had emerged a victor. And much more was written about her than the child who ultimately won the spelling bee.

Being a person of truth, even when the truth hurts, brings the greatest and most lasting rewards.

Them that honour me I will honour.

1 SAMUEL 2:30

References

Unless otherwise indicated, all Scripture quotations are taken from the *King James Version* of the Bible.

Scripture quotations marked NIV are taken from the *Holy Bible, New International Version*® NIV®. Copyright © 1973, 1978, 1984 by International Bible Society. Used by permission of Zondervan Publishing House. All Rights reserved.

Scripture quotations marked NASB are taken from the *New American Standard Bible.* Copyright © the Lockman Foundation 1960, 1962, 1963, 1968, 1971, 1972, 1973, 1975, 1977, 1995. Used by permission.

Scripture quotations marked AMP are taken from *The Amplified Bible, Old Testament,* Copyright © 1965, 1986 by Zondervan Publishing House, Grand Rapids, Michigan. *New Testament* copyright © 1958, 1987 by The Lockman Foundation, La Habra, California. Used by permission.

Scripture quotations marked NKJV are taken from *The New King James Version of the Bible.* Copyright © 1979, 1980, 1982, 1994 by Thomas Nelson, Inc., Publishers. Used by permission.

Verses marked TLB are taken from *The Living Bible,* copyright © 1971. Used by permission of Tyndale House Publishers, Inc., Wheaton, Illinois 60189. All rights reserved.

Acknowledgements

Ruth Bell Graham (8), Mother Teresa (10,48,252), Jean Hodges (12), George M. Adams (16), Helen Pearson (22), Joseph Addison (24), Cyrus (26), Henry Ward Beecher (28), G.W.C. Thomas (34), Betty Mills (36), Josh Billings (38, 248), Thackeray (40), Joyce Heinrich and Annettee La Placa (42), Joyce Earline Steelburg (44), St. Basil (46), Catherine Graham (78), Lillian Dickson (80), Cervantes (82), Sebastian-Roche (84), Mark Twain (88,216,224), William James (90), Zig Ziglar (94), William Feather (96) Bill Cosby (98), Charles Dickens (100), Euripedes (104), Martin Luther King Jr. (106), William Carey (108), Benjamin Franklin (110), Dennis Waitley (116), Mary Gardner Brainard (120), Walt Disney (122), Arnold H. Glasgow (208), Mort Walker (210), Richard Exley (212), John Newton (218), Mark Steele (220), Olin Miller (230), Joseph P. Dooley (236), June Henderson (244), Dr. John Olson (246), Reverend Larry Lorenzoni (256), James Howell (258), Ralph Waldo Emerson (260), Charles H. Spurgeon (226), George Herbert Palmer (268), Thomas Jefferson (270), Jim Elliot (272), Doug Larsen (274), Elton Trueblood (276), Ivern Ball (286), Merceline Cox (290), Henry Ford (294), Mary Pickford (298), Thomas Edison (300), Charles E. Hummell (304), Eleanor Roosevelt (306).

Endnotes

[1] *Words to Love By,* Mother Teresa (Notre Dame, IN : Ave Maria Press, 1983), pp. 55, 59.

[2] *Especially for a Woman,* Ann Kiemel Anderson (Nashville, TN: Thomas Nelson Publishers, 1994), p. 42.

[3] *Illustrations for Preaching and Teaching,* Craig Brian Larson, ed. (Grand Rapids, MI: Baker Books, 1993), p. 119.

[4] "That's What Friends Are For," by Jane Gross, Ladies Home Journal, July 1995, p. 146.

[5] *Family Circle,* September 1, 1995, p. 114.

[6] *Little House in the Ozarks,* Laura Ingalls Wilder (Nashville, TN: Thomas Nelson Publishers, 1991), p.36.

[7] *A Closer Walk,* Catherine Marshall (Grand Rapids, MI: Fleming H. Revell, Division of Baker book House Co., 1986), p.87-88.

[8] *People,* March 20, 1995, pp. 87-88.

[9] *Dakota,* Kathleen Norris, (New York, NY: Houghton Mifflin, 1993), p. 114.

[10] *TV Guide,* July 22 1995, p. 29.

[11] "Anatomy of a Champion," George Sheehan, Runner's World, May 1993, p. 18.

[12] *Learning to Forgive,* Doris Donnelly (New York, NY: Macmillan Publishing, 1979), pp. 24-25.

[13] *Newsweek,* April 24, 1995, p. 150.

[14] *Let Me Illustrate,* Albert P. Stauderman (Minneapolis, MN: Augsburg Press, 1983), p. 104.

[15] "Of Love and Loss," Jennet Conant, *Redbook,* October 1994, p. 82.

16 *Illustrations for Preaching and Teaching,* Craig Brian Larson, ed. (Grand Rapids, MI: Baker Books, 1993), p. 200.

17 *Decision,* September 1995, p. 4-5.

18 *Little House in the Ozarks,* Laura Ingalls Wilder (Nashville, TN: Thomas Nelson Publishers, 1991), p. 103.

19 "Signs and Wonders," John Garvey, *Commonweal,* April 22, 1994, p. 10.

20 "By Faith Not Sight," Ruth A. Morgan, *Encyclopedia of 7700 Illustrations,* Paul Lee Tan, ed. (Rockville, MD: Assurance Publishers, 1979), p. 404.

21 "I Know Something Good About You," *Knight's Master Book of New Illustrations,* Walter B. Knight (Grand Rapids, MI: Eerdmans Pub. Co., 1956), pp. 174-175.

22 "Disaster Weddings and How Couples Coped," Barbara Rachel Pollack, Redbook, August 1995, p. 102.

23 *Growing Strong in the Seasons of Life,* Charles Swindoll (Portland, OR: Multnomah Press, 1983), p. 100.

24 "Mottoes," Kalends, *The New Speaker's Treasury of Wit and Wisdom,* Herbert V. Prochnow, ed. (New York, NY: Harper & Row, 1958), p. 290.

25 *Little House in the Ozarks,* Laura Ingalls Wilder (Nashville, TN: Thomas Nelson Publishers, 1991), p. 68.

26 Author and title of poem unknown. Found in *Speaker's Encyclopedia of Stories, Quotations, and Anecdotes,* Jacob M. Braude (Englewood Cliffs, NJ: Prentice-Hall, 1955), p. 307.

27 Story from *Illustrations Unlimited,* James Hewett, ed. (Wheaton, IL: Tyndale House Publishers, 1988), pp. 131-132.

28 *Illustrations for Preaching and Teaching,* Craig Brian Larson, ed. (Grand Rapids, MI: Baker Books, 1993), p. 97.

29 *Illustrations for Preaching and Teaching,* Craig Brian Larson, ed. (Grand Rapids, MI: Baker Books, 1993), p. 187.

30 *It's My Turn,* Ruth Bell Graham (Minneapolis, MN: Grason, 1982), p. 110.

31 "Janette Oke: Pioneer Novelist," Nancy McGough, *Homelife,* November 1995, pp. 12, 14-15.

32 "A Character Quiz," Herbert V. Prochnow, *The Speaker's Book of Illustrations,* Herbert V. Prochnow, ed. (Grand Rapids, MI: Baker Book House, 1960), p. 100.

33 *A Lamp For My Feet,* Elizabeth Elliot (Ann Arbor, MI: Servant Publications, 1987), p. 52.

34 *Illustrations for Preaching and Teaching,* Craig Brian Larson, ed. (Grand Rapids, MI: Baker Books, 1993), p. 250-251.

35 *Especially for a Woman,* Beverly LaHaye (Nashville, TN: Thomas Nelson, 1994), p. 253, 263.

Additional copies of this book and other
titles in the *God's Little Devotional Book* series
are available from your local bookstore.
Also look for our
Special Gift Editions in this series.

God's Little Devotional Book
God's Little Devotional Book for Men
God's Little Devotional Book for the Moms
God's Little Devotional Book for Dads
God's Little Devotional Book for Students
God's Little Devotional Book for Graduates
God's Little Devotional Book for Teachers
God's Little Devotional Book for Teens

If you have enjoyed this book,
or if it has impacted your life,
we would like to hear from you.

Please contact us at:

Honor Books
4050 Lee Vance View
Colorado Springs, Colorado 80918